Back on Track

How to Straighten Out Your Life When It Throws You a Curve

DEBORAH NORVILLE

SIMON & SCHUSTER

SIMON & SCHUSTER
Rockefeller Center
1230 Avenue of the Americas
New York, NY 10020

Copyright © 1997 by Deborah Norville

SIMON & SCHUSTER and colophon are registered trademarks
of Simon & Schuster Inc.

Designed by Irving Perkins Associates

Manufactured in the United States of America

10 9 8 7 6 5 4 3 2 1

Library of Congress Cataloging-in-Publication Data

Norville, Deborah.
    Back on track: how to straighten out your life when it throws you
a curve/Deborah Norville
        p.   cm.
    1. Women—Conduct of life. 2. Women—Life skills guides. 3. Life
change events. 4. Norville, Deborah. I. Title.
BJ1610.N67   1997
158'.082—dc21   97-9586
                                                             CIP

ISBN 0-684-83260-7

To the men in my life:

Karl, Niki, and Kyle

Acknowledgments

THIS BOOK REPRESENTS THE COMPLETION of a journey—and I hope the beginning of another. There are many people to whom I am very grateful. Some of them I must mention here.

Karl. You believed in me when it seemed the world hated me. When you tried to track down one nasty columnist to punch his nose, I was glad you couldn't find him—but I love you for trying!

To Niki and Kyle for giving me the *real* perspective on life.

To the greatest sisters in the world who've been there through thick and thin. I would love you even if we weren't related.

Daddy, you set the example that hard work *does* pay off—and never cut me any slack when I wanted it!

To that "literary expert" who told me I shouldn't write this book, thank *you*. Your rejection gave me the renewed faith that led me to Jan Miller, my literary agent who has always "gotten it."

To Carolyn Reidy, Michele Martin, and Dominick Anfuso at Simon & Schuster who also "get it." They knew instantly the story I wanted to tell and helped me share it with you.

Thanks to my assistant, Tiffany Johns, for helping me track down things and generally helping to keep me and my life in order!

To the brave women—some named, some pseudonymous—who allowed me to share their stories and to the thousands who've attended my speeches and shared with me afterward, a special hug. *You* helped me get back on track.

And to my mom. I wish you were here to share this. I hope you're proud. I really, really miss you.

CONTENTS

Introduction

THE COMEBACK KID

Sᴏᴍᴇᴏɴᴇ ᴏɴᴄᴇ ᴀsᴋᴇᴅ ᴍᴇ ʜᴏᴡ I'd like my tombstone to read. I hoped this wasn't a question in need of an imminent answer . . . but I thought about it. "Comeback Kid" would be nice, I replied—because that is how I feel in so many ways. Like I've made a comeback. A resurrection. For all intents and purposes, I was dead and buried professionally speaking. And yet—I'm here.

Five years ago my career was over. I was out of network television. Out of television altogether. I was fat. I weighed . . . well, there are some things that a lady just doesn't *ever* disclose. But put it this way: my husband's jeans wouldn't come close to even going over my thighs. To be described as zaftig would have been kind!

I'd been pilloried in the press as the "other woman," called "hungry as a shark," and parodied on *Saturday Night Live* as Eve Harrington from *All About* . . .

Even Johnny Carson had a go at me. "Tom Brokaw is in Berlin covering the tearing down of the wall," he'd joked. "He'd better watch out. Deborah Norville's been seen throwing banana peels behind him."

It was funny. But it hurt.

● ● ●

So here I was: March 1991. I'd worked almost nonstop in television since I was nineteen years old, a college kid. And yet I was now—out of work. And no one, not even I, would have put much money on a bet that I'd ever be back.

Out of work. What a weird way to describe yourself when you come from a family where work is just part and parcel of the average day. That was me. Unemployed. Mother of a four-week-old. Paralyzed by depression. In need of a career—and without the inner strength to try to find one.

And yet, fast-forward: March 1996. Five years later. I've now got two children, so yummy you could eat them. I'm back in size six skirts. Reasonably in shape. *And*—hosting the most successful news magazine show in syndication.

How did this happen? It's a question that I ask myself with pride. Because I know the answer came from within. I did it myself.

Funny that I write that. I did it myself. I can hear my own voice saying that same phrase, yet it's a little girl's voice. High with the shrillness of childhood, filled with the pride of the words. Since I was a kid, I've been saying, "I can do that myself."

I think in a way, the desire to "do it myself" has been a curse. I'm unwilling to delegate. It's not that I can do it better, but I get it done faster. It takes time for me to explain what I want done. I get impatient. "I can do it" has long been my motto—and now I hear my own little boy saying the same thing!

And yet, "I can do it myself" may be what got me here. No one else could have dragged me out of the abyss into which I fell after leaving television—for good, as I thought at the time. I crawled my way back, one painful day at a time.

How many of you have had a crisis in your life?

How many of you have felt yourself severely depressed?

Have you ever shoveled food in your face when you were hurt or angry and hated yourself at the time for doing it?

Have you ever eaten to get back at someone else who has hurt or angered you?

How many of you have looked at your house, your healthy kids, your spouse and *really* felt sorry for yourself?

Have you ever had the sense that life is just a series of days strung together? You just plod through them and at some point it all ends?

You were having a crisis. Just like me.

The difference was that my crisis played itself out there for all of America to see.

I'm sure there were some people who tuned in to the *Today* show when I was there just to see if I was crying. Wasn't Deborah a bit red around the eyes? No, I wasn't, to answer you. I never let them see me cry. Which isn't to say I didn't shed tears. Plenty of them!

My bosses said, "Be yourself on the air." Yet the producer also said, "Don't speak unless Bryant talks to you first."

The driver in the morning would tell me whether it was safe to read the papers or not. There were a lot of mornings the papers went unread because of some vicious articles about me.

Sometimes we would go to work via the garage under Rockefeller Center. That was on the days when *Hard Copy* or *A Current Affair* would be waiting to ambush me at four A.M. I probably should have let them see me. The way I look at four in the morning, it would have dispelled the glamour gal/homewrecker image real fast!

My crisis was professional. But it could be: your husband comes home and says he's in love—and it's not with you.

Your child has a dreadful illness and the doctors aren't sure how to treat it.

A freak accident leaves you—or someone you love—terribly injured and your life will never be the same.

It is the curveball that life throws you that sends you reeling.

You didn't see it coming so you couldn't be prepared for it. Or maybe the signs were there, but your head was in the sand and you didn't read them. Either way, you've been psychologically punched in the gut and left gasping for air.

The good news is you don't have to stay down for the count. You may have gotten hit with a sucker punch, but until the referee counts ten, the match isn't over. Great, you say, but I'm the one who's down here on the mat, Deborah, not you. Well, honey, I've been there too! And think of this as you're lying there on the ground (or in the gutter or wherever you visualize yourself as being): there's only one way to go, and that's up. This book is designed to help you get there.

Believe it or not, you *can* change the course your life is taking. You may not be able to change the doctor's diagnosis. You might not be able to make your husband love you again. But you can love yourself. You can get back that self-esteem that's lost from you now. You can see life as worth living. You can *like* yourself again.

Don't think so? Neither did Jana when she was paralyzed in a car accident. Neither did Ruth when diagnosed with breast cancer. Or Marcia when she was raped. Or Robin whose marriage fell apart. Or Cynthia when she and her husband lost everything.

Joan saw no bright future when her husband committed suicide. Nor could Susie when her sons were diagnosed with a terrible disease. Christina was devastated by a series of miscarriages. And imagine being Caye and receiving the news that your husband is among the victims of the Oklahoma City bombing.

I wish I could say, "Follow the simple steps in this book and those goals will be yours." But I'd be misleading you. It's like the commercial Cher did a few years ago for an exercise club: "Great bodies. If they came in a bottle, everyone would have one."

The steps may seem simple, but taking them is not. What I hope I *can* do is encourage you to try walking. And I hope that by sharing my story and those of some other courageous women who've gotten back on track, you'll find within you the inspiration and the strength to take those first steps.

You can feel good about yourself. You can enjoy your life. When I look back on where I was after my NBC days—"used her up, . . . dumped her in a ditch and left her for dead" as the *Chicago Tribune* described it—I feel pretty good about where I am. You can too. Good luck, I'm praying for you.

Chapter One

GOODBYE MISS SCARLETT

"I won't think about that today. I'll think about that tomorrow."

—Scarlett O'Hara, in *Gone With the Wind,* by Margaret Mitchell

How OFTEN HAVE YOU HAD something unpleasant you had to deal with, and you decided to procrastinate? Put it off. Deal with it later. "Think about that tomorrow." You know you've got to speak with a colleague at work whose performance is off and you know it's not going to be pleasant. Put it off one more day. It won't make that much difference, right?

It's a funny thing about crisis. We all know chances are pretty good that at some point in our life we'll be confronted by a crisis, but we don't do much to get ready for it. Think back. Did your mother or father ever school you in how to deal with a crisis when it hits?

I'm not talking about being taught to put a lid on a grease fire when you're cooking bacon. Or how to call 911 when the burglars are sneaking in the window. Good for you if you know CPR and have your Red Cross certification. You've prepared yourself for an *emergency*. But that's different from a *crisis*.

An emergency is short-lived. Your adrenaline kicks in and your body reacts by instinct or by training to handle the situation. A crisis lasts longer and hits deeper. Its onset may be instantaneous—your husband is injured in an automobile accident—or the crisis could be a long time in developing—your marriage started deteriorating months or even years ago, but only now is the fabric of your relationship ripping.

Common sense tells us it's highly unlikely that we'll manage to get through a lifetime without some sort of debacle. A few individuals do have those charmed existences. But I've never been one of those kinds of lucky people.

My front tooth was knocked out when I was eight years old. When I was ten, I found out I was blind as a bat and had to wear glasses. And throughout my childhood, I always saw myself as the fat, ugly kid in class. I never won anything as a kid until I was nearly out of high school. Well, I won one thing: I Bingo'ed when I was about ten years old on spring vacation. I won a thermos and a lunchbox. Wow!

Most of all, my childhood was marked by repeated episodes during which my mother spent weeks at a time in the hospital. First, there was her spinal surgery when I was eight, then she was diagnosed with rheumatoid arthritis when I was eleven. By the time I reached high school, my parents were divorcing and Momma was confined to a wheelchair.

What I knew about dealing with adversity was largely what I'd observed watching my mom bravely, yet privately, confront that body of hers that just never seemed to work quite right. My sisters and I were her "arms and legs," as she put it, who helped her run the household.

Oddly enough, I never had a heart-to-heart with Momma about how she got through the undeserved physical failings that she seemed to deal with on a daily basis. She just—coped. Then again, maybe those are questions one doesn't think to ask as a teenager. When I was old enough to ask them, Momma was gone. She died when I was twenty.

Equally surprising—even though I'd lived through my mom's

struggle with two devastating situations, divorce and chronic illness—it never occurred to me to consider what *I* would do if a calamity came into my own life directly. I think very few of us do that.

While we know life's not likely to spare us a few unpleasantries, how much do we prepare for it? How much do our parents talk with us about the possibility of our foundation being really shaken somewhere down the line? They're more apt to explain the birds and the bees before they address ways to cope with or avoid crisis. And we *all* know how eager parents are to talk about sex with their kids!

When I was eleven, they showed us the movie about menstruation at school. I came home and told my mother they'd showed us "that movie." She said, "Did they give you any books to read?"

I said they had. In fact, I'd managed to hang on to mine. The fifth-grade boys were offering *serious* money to buy those books from us girls.

Mom said, "Well, when you've finished reading them, we'll sit down and talk about it."

That was in 1969. We never did have that conversation.

We never had a conversation about coping with crisis either.

Where I come from in Georgia, there are two "good books." The Bible and *Gone With the Wind*. Mind you, there are still pickup trucks in my part of Georgia where the gun rack is visible and well stocked and the guy behind the wheel isn't kidding about that bumper sticker on the back that reads, "Forgit HELL!" with a rebel flag on it.

Both books have had enormous influence on me. To me, my debutante dress looks a bit like the off-the-shoulder number Scarlett was wearing when she was flirting with all those Southern boys at the Wilkes plantation the day war was declared.

I think all of us are a lot like Scarlett in ways that we probably wish we weren't. I know I am.

When it comes to thinking about the possibility of having a serious crisis to contend with, when it comes to plotting a strategy to dealing with that inevitable future disaster, we turn into Scarlett. "Why," we declare to ourselves, "I'll think about that tomorrow!"

We push out of our minds the disagreeable prospect of having our lives turned topsy-turvy to another time when we'll be better able to think about it.

"I'm busy," we say to ourselves.

"Life is so good right now," we remind ourselves. "I don't want to jinx it by thinking about things going wrong."

"I'm a good person. God wouldn't let something really horrible happen."

We have a million excuses to avoid thinking about the unpleasant possibility of our world being overturned. We'll take first-aid classes to be able to save a life. Learn defensive driving to avoid an accident. Take special training to improve our standing at work. But we avoid like the plague doing a little preplanning and a lot of soul searching about how we'd cope with a crisis.

Like Scarlett O'Hara we tell ourselves, "I won't think about that today. I'll think about that tomorrow."

Well, my tomorrow came at *Today.*

I had always had a charmed life in television. After testing out of my freshman year in college, I landed a terrific internship with Georgia Public Television my second year at the University of Georgia. Those were the days before C-SPAN, when cameras were a rarity at state legislatures.

I, along with three other coeds from Georgia, wrote, reported, and anchored a daily program called *The Lawmakers.* It was a show which chronicled the daily action (and *that's* using the word *very* loosely) of the Georgia House and Senate. It was hardly riveting television: could *you* really watch twenty-two minutes of debate over which company should provide the stuff that makes license plates reflective? Those were the burning issues that filled our hour-long program.

And yet, the last day of the legislative session—the last day of our internship—the wife of the man who ran the CBS television station in Atlanta was flipping channels, saw me, and called her husband over to the television. For some reason, Shelly Schwab saw a hint of television potential.

Two months later, I was interning at his station, WAGA-TV in Atlanta. The third day I was there, the assignment desk was low on reporters—and just like that scene in the Broadway musical *42nd Street,* I got the call.

"Miss Norville . . . ? You're on!"

Well, it wasn't exactly like that. Actually, someone shouted, "Hey, Norville, go cover this damn picnic!"

Either way, it was television and that night I was on the six o'-clock news. It was a feature on the local fire department's family picnic. Again, not exactly riveting television—but hey, that was *me* on the screen!

And so it went. I reported for the station every day. Some of the stories were challenging: I covered the arrest of a gang of gas station operators who were ripping off motorists on their way through Georgia. Others were eminently forgettable: was that really me pretending to talk like a baby zebra when the Atlanta zoo's latest addition was paraded before the public? When summer ended, my news director offered me a deal: if I'd work weekends as a reporter, they'd guarantee me a reporting job when I was graduated the following June.

Wow! Like there was really a decision to make? I was thrilled to say yes.

And so I worked my butt off. Driving the hour it took to reach Atlanta from the university in Athens. Sometimes I would sleep over at a friend's apartment, borrowing the living room couch. But often, there wasn't room at the friend's and I didn't always have enough money for a hotel room. Those were the times I would sleep in my car.

I was very nervous about sleeping in my car. Partly I was terrified some ax murderer would come and get me. So I'd park under a street lamp at an apartment complex not far from the station. It would have been much safer to park at the station and sleep there, but I was worried someone would recognize my car and think I was "catting around." Worse—someone might find me in the back seat! How *mortifying*! So, I'd sleep in the back seat and sneak into the station in the morning to get dressed, do my makeup, and be ready to play TV reporter.

I don't know if sleeping in my car had anything to do with it, but the hard work seemed to be paying off: One columnist called me "The Golden Girl." *Atlanta Magazine* referred to the college kid working as an on-air TV reporter as an "anomaly." Heavens, I was only nineteen when I got to do a live interview with the president of the United States! I was the first to admit, it *did* seem a charmed existence for a kid trying to break into such a cutthroat business.

I became the weekend news anchor when I was graduated from college. When Jimmy Carter left the White House and the Atlanta child murders case was solved, it seemed time to leave the safety of my home state. I headed north to where the Yankees lived.

Chicago had then, and still does, the reputation for being the best local news market in the country. It had two city papers and several suburban newspapers which were every bit as competitive as the *Tribune* and the *Sun-Times*. And the television reporters were just as good at breaking the big story as the print folks.

At risk of offending my husband, I'll tell *you* my five years in Chicago were among the best in my life. I was only twenty-three when I moved up there (in January . . . which, coupled with my blonde hair and my Southern accent, only confirmed I was a real airhead. *No one* moves to Chicago in January!). And—I made plenty of mistakes. I mistook a car dealer for a U.S. senator—that one didn't get on the air. And got the tax assessor confused with the head of the Tax Appeals Board—that one did—on *live* television. But generally, the audience liked me and I felt my colleagues at WMAQ, Channel 5, thought I belonged.

That had always been my goal in going to Chicago. The best reporters were there. If I could hold my own with that bunch, then maybe I *did* belong in television news.

Then I got the call to come to New York and join NBC News as the anchor of *News at Sunrise,* their early morning news program. I could hardly believe my good luck. Maybe that Golden Girl stuff was right. The truth was, I'd decided I was coming to New York long before the NBC job materialized. I'd been dating this guy . . . this really *neat* guy . . . who lived in New York. His business kept him from being able to move and my contract was up in Chicago, so it looked like I'd be the one doing the moving. (That "neat guy" is now my husband. Smart move, don't you think?)

Anchoring *Sunrise* was a joy. Even though the hours probably violate the Constitution's prohibition against "cruel and unusual punishment"—no one should go to work at 2:30 in the morning!—the job was a dream. The producers and writers were friendly, funny, and terribly smart. Every day I felt I learned something. And, since we were the first newscast "out of the chute," we felt that *Sunrise* helped to set the agenda for the day.

Of course, sometimes, I didn't always set it properly. Whenever we'd run across a town or name whose pronunciation we were unsure about, we'd usually try to call and get the correct pronunciation. But it wasn't always possible.

"Say it with authority" was our motto. If you say it like you're sure you're right, the audience will think you are. It didn't always work. How were we to know that town in Alaska was called Val-DEEZ instead of Val-dez? And you can bet, people called to correct me.

It was an amazing time to anchor the early morning news. We knew before most of America woke up that the stock market was about to have an awful day. It was four A.M. our time when the Tokyo stock market tanked one October morning. We saw the '87 market crash coming before it happened. Later, we'd literally watch communism disintegrate before our eyes. As one East European nation after another saw democracy rise and communism fall, we started to get slap-happy. "Quick," we'd joke. "What's the capital city of Albania? Looks like they're next!" (It's Tirana, if you're wondering.)

A side benefit of anchoring *Sunrise* was the occasional opportunity to fill in on the *Today* show. Terror doesn't begin to describe what I felt before my first stint as a substitute!

The fear began on Friday before the Monday broadcast. It started when I got the rundown of what was planned for the show. It was then that I learned my first interview would be with Yuli Vorontzov, the Soviet arms negotiator. Oh my God! If I screw this up, I could start a nuclear war. I'd never felt so inadequate in all my life.

But the interview with Yuli went without creating a nuclear conflagration. The Cold War ended. And the folks at NBC asked me time and again to fill in for Jane Pauley and, on occasion, Bryant Gumbel.

I remember Jane's words of welcome: "I'm so glad you're here. Now I can be sick sometimes!" And indeed, there were times when I'd be on the computer at three A.M. writing my script for *Sunrise* when Jane would electronically message, "Aside from the headache and throwing up part, could you be me for today?"

It was a nice arrangement. I had the safety of *Sunrise* where we did lots of live reports and breaking stories—my greatest joy in television. And I had the fun of doing *Today*. I'd gotten over my jitters. Once I realized that it isn't brain surgery, it was actually quite fun. Besides, since I was an occasional substitute, it meant I could sneak into the Green Room where guests were asked to wait. They had the *best* chocolate chip cookies in the world in there! It's probably what I miss most from NBC.

There were some fun times during that period. I recall one show just before Christmas when I was filling in for Bryant. We were doing a "Twelve Days of Christmas" series of gift ideas, and on this particular day the topic was gifts for a cook. I was supposed to talk about the gadgets while Jane played sidekick.

Things got rough right off the bat. The first gizmo was an overnight bread maker. The crust was so tough Jane couldn't begin to saw through it. I left her hacking away and moved on to show the audience a newfangled microwave coffee maker—it supposedly made fresh-brewed coffee in seconds.

Earlier, I'd spent a lot of time learning how to work this gadget: where to put the coffee, the water, etc. But it never occurred to me to check out the microwave. Well, as Jane was hacking away, I am standing there totally defeated by the microwave. I couldn't figure out how to open the darned thing!

By this point, Jane and I realize all of America have decided we are the two dumbest blondes in the country. We cut to a break during which time a studio stagehand sawed the bread and made the coffee, which frankly looked a bit watery. Jane tried to show the weak coffee to the audience when the break was over and instead dumped it all over the suede desktop. (I figured that desktop probably cost a few thousand dollars.)

The next day, someone had put a sign on my door that said "Ethel" and Jane had one that read "Lucy." It *was* a lot of fun!

Still, no one could have been more surprised than I was in August of 1989 when I got a call from Dick Ebersol. He was the president of NBC Sports, who for some reason had been given the *Today* show as part of his purview. I'd played basketball in high school, but I didn't think that was why he was calling. Unless catalogue browsing was becoming a sport, I just didn't see what about me would be of interest to him.

What he wanted to tell me was that I'd been tapped to be the news anchor on *Today*. The plan according to Ebersol was that John Palmer and I would switch jobs—he'd go to *Sunrise* and I'd move over to *Today*. They wanted more live reporter debriefs and evidently the bosses liked the way I did that sort of thing on *Sunrise*.

"What do Jane and Bryant think about this?" was my first question.

"Well, they're obviously sad for John, but they think it's best for the show," was Ebersol's reply. He went on to say something about them saying they enjoyed working with me.

A job on the *Today* show was at the time probably one of the pinnacles in broadcast television. It was the top-rated morning show, the granddaddy of the genre. It was not something you turn down.

That August was a pretty amazing month. First, I was offered the job of *Today* news anchor and a couple of weeks later a documentary I'd done on violent teenage girls was an astonishing ratings success. I was fairly certain the title the advertising department had picked had something to do with it. No doubt a good number of people tuned in to "Bad Girls" thinking of the old Donna Summer song and expecting to see girls in tight shorts with their bottoms hanging out!

Instead, what they got was an hour of television about girls who were so frighteningly violent and so amazingly blasé about it the viewers couldn't change the channel. Who wouldn't be glued to the tube when a teenager from Massachusetts talks about how cool it was to open someone's car door and slam a baseball bat in their face for kicks? "Bad Girls" ranked number seven in that week's Nielsen ratings. Someone told me it was the highest rating *any* television news documentary had ever gotten at that time.

I guess to some folks, I was having it a little too good.

One article had pegged me NBC's "fastest rising star." I guess someone decided to take the "star" down a few pegs. The next thing I knew, a few weeks later, I was being called "hungry as a shark" and open season on Deborah Norville had apparently begun.

There was a steady drumbeat of stories that rapidly became a crescendo of character assassination. If this were a tell-all book, I'd offer my theories about who caused it and how it all happened. But I'm beyond that. What happened happened.

All I know is I accepted the job my bosses had offered me. Sat where they told me to sit. Then—suddenly *I'd* become the woman who'd wrecked the happy home called the *Today* show. (I can't help but think parenthetically, how happy was it, anyway? Didn't those reporters remember that awful computer memo that someone filched from Bryant's file?)

When we sold our apartment, I found a couple of file boxes filled with clips from that time. After a while, I stopped reading. From being the "rising star" at the network, I'd become "The Other Woman" in one newspaper's headline. A magazine writer used my last name as a verb: to be "norvilled" meant to be unfairly pushed out of your job. That hurt worst, I think. How dare they take my family name and disparage it. My father was a self-made man who *earned* his success in business. Through my parents' example, I'd seen how hard work and tenacity could pay off. And I'd made my way in television without a famous family or any connections. Yet some woman whose job it is to talk about people tries to sully my family name. It was the lowest possible blow. As I said, I stopped reading the clips.

But reading those old stories helped me realize just how far I'd come since those days when it seemed I was tethered to a merry-go-round that just seemed to whirl faster and faster. I hadn't asked to get on and so I couldn't figure out how to get off the whirlwind. It was also a reminder of just how bad the situation had been.

The gist of the stories was that I was somehow finagling Jane Pauley's ouster. And yet, in the midst of the furor, she sent a computer note to me: "I am so very sorry to have complicated your life as I have. . . . [I've told a reporter that] there's been speculation that deborah norville [*sic*] is the centerpiece of these discussions. this [*sic*] is not the case. . . ."

Jane's note was awfully nice to read on the computer at 5:40 A.M. But it seemed that the press would not pick up on this end of the story.

The stories began getting worse . . . going from "sordid details" of how I was "plotting" against Jane to unfounded speculation in a supermarket tabloid that it was romantic infatuation on the part of NBC head Bob Wright that had led to my promotion. One female columnist opined that I "could easily have been the high school tramp, taking on the entire football team while still acing calculus and biology." That same column included a comment from some guy who seemed to have a problem with my religious beliefs (I accepted Christ as my savior when I was fifteen). He said, "She's got this born again rap. . . . She should be stopped immediately!"

Just going through the old news clips to retrieve that quote for this brought back that old horrible sense of paralysis and the involuntary shiver I would go through each time another press barrage came my way.

What was so bizarre to me was how quickly my position at

Today seemed to have changed. When I'd fill in as a substitute, there was a rapport with the other cast members that was really quite warm. Staffers had commented to me about the "chemistry" between Bryant and me.

And I knew Bryant had been a big supporter of mine. You didn't get the chance to substitute without Bryant's approval—after all, he was the one who had to work with Jane's fill-in. And more than once, he'd been wonderfully gracious. The morning I told my NBC colleagues that Karl and I had gotten engaged, Bryant playfully announced our news to the whole country.

During those initial weeks of horrible articles, Bryant sent me a computer message: "Hang tough . . . you're not alone . . . and I won't desert you."

It was a huge comfort to receive that message—and yet, it was the only expression of support he ever sent my way. I couldn't figure out why someone who had been a champion of mine, seemed unable or unwilling to come to my defense.

Years later, someone asked me, "Where was Bryant during all of this? Didn't he ever offer you some advice?" I suppose he was in a position to come to my aid, but that never happened—nor was it something I would have expected.

As much as I was hoping that someone would speak up for me, or at least, bark at some of the reporters who seemed to be making stories up out of whole cloth, I had no expectation that would occur. I was alone. And I knew it.

I remember vividly going to the woman who was the head of communications for NBC at the time and begging her to let me respond to the reports. My assistant had two legal-sized pages filled with the names of reporters who wanted to talk to me.

And yet, I was under a gag order. "Don't talk to the press, Deborah," was what I was told. "Let us handle this," she said. "We're experts at this."

I'll share my thoughts about "experts" with you a bit later!

The reporters assumed my silence meant I was avoiding them. The experts at NBC thought that to dignify the sordid stories with any kind of reply would lead the reporters to do *more* stories. To my way of thinking, *not* to respond only gave them the green light to do more of the same. Hindsight's 20/20—but I think *I* was right.

My instinct told me to respond. To stand up for myself. It might not make them stop printing ugly stories about me, but it might plant the seed in the back of their minds and make them hesitate a bit knowing, "We'll hear about this one."

I think the clearest sign that leaving this in the hands of the experts was a *big* mistake was the lunch I had with one of NBC's outside public relations experts. He was with a fancy firm retained by General Electric, NBC's parent company, to "handle" the whole mess. I asked him what he'd thought of that day's broadcast—did I seem relaxed, what did he think of a particular interview? He had to admit he hadn't watched the show that day. I pressed on. "Well, what about yesterday?"

He had to confess, after I started going back in time, day by day, that he hadn't seen *any* of the *Today* show programs in the near month since I'd come on as co-host! And NBC and its corporate parent, General Electric, were paying significant dollars to this company for "public relations counsel"? *That* was scary.

That was the first of what I later realized were a number of signs that this new "home" on *Today* wasn't going to be very hospitable.

Actually, to be fair, I'd already been given a sign that this *Today* gig wasn't going to be all it was cracked up to be. When the co-host torch was passed to me by Jane Pauley, it was done during a very emotional segment on the program. Jane said Barbara Walters had wished her good luck and a good alarm clock—and she then presented me with a little clock.

Turns out, the alarm clock was broken! Jane apologized about it later, saying it had gotten banged up when she and Bryant had rushed to San Francisco to cover the earthquake.

Years later, when I was able to laugh about the whole debacle, I couldn't help but chuckle over the irony. The broken clock seemed to be a metaphor for the entire *Today* experience.

I remember trying to set up meetings with some of the senior-level producers. I was pregnant at the time and exhausted. But they said they'd be available around noon or 12:30 P.M. I waited and waited. No one showed up for the meeting, so finally I went in search of the three folks I was supposed to meet. One had left the building, another had gone to the cafeteria to eat, and the third was nowhere to be found. I'd been stiffed—and no one had the courtesy to tell me they weren't planning to show up. "I forgot!" was what I was told later.

No one ever said television was a nice business. And when you work at the network level, you know it's going to be cutthroat. I remember when I was leaving WMAQ-TV in Chicago to join the network someone advised me to walk down the hall like a crab: "Keep your back covered," they warned. I came to New York understandably nervous and yet when I got there, I found the people I worked with warm, friendly, and professional. I later realized the halls I'd been walking in as anchor of *Sunrise* had been the safe ones. This new route I was taking was chock-full of boobytraps.

I guess that's what made the shock of what happened at *Today* all the more intense. At *Sunrise* there wasn't time for anyone to be Machiavellian. We were all sleep-deprived and just struggling to get the show on the air. When things didn't work, when machines broke down, we'd tap-dance around the situation and make it look okay. Most of the time the audience never knew there had been a problem.

And the camaraderie was wonderful. By ten o'clock, we'd often be down at Hurley's bar on the corner. Yes, we'd put a little something extra in our coffee! After all, when you'd get up at the time we did, it *was* cocktail hour.

Today was different. At *Today*, I felt so alone. The people who'd been so warm and welcoming to me as a fill-in substitute now seemed to blame me for the bad press the program was getting. And yes, the ratings did take a header.

"Jeez," I'd say to myself. "I didn't ask for this stupid job!" Sometimes Dick Ebersol would try to comfort me. "Just save it for the book," he'd say. What he didn't realize, I guess, is that I did. I kept a diary. But that's not a book I'll ever publish. I know what it's like to be hurt. I'm not interested in passing those hurts along.

Hammurabi's Law of an "Eye for an eye and a tooth for a tooth" may have been fine for ancient Babylon, but it's not for Deborah Norville.

For a while, I tried to turn it around. One magazine had printed a snipey little piece about how supposedly folks on the show were calling me "the stewardess" because I was so "peppy" around the office. Well! I could think of lots worse things to be called. But this wasn't meant as a compliment.

So, I asked my assistant, Lynn, to help me and together we gathered little boxes of raisins, some coffee pots, and cups. I borrowed a seat belt from the stagehands and a necktie from the wardrobe mistress. Then I marched into a staff meeting with "NBC peacock wings" and launched into the whole flight attendant routine about putting your tray tables in their locked position and gave the seat belt lecture and served coffee. I wanted the staff to know that I wasn't going to let the press get me down and didn't want them to get bummed out either. (The "experts" had said I couldn't talk to the press, but they hadn't banned me from talking to my co-workers! At least not *yet*.) Everyone had a chuckle. I don't recall that my stewardess "act" ever was reported by the magazine that had published the earlier article!

It was hopeless.

When I became pregnant, the media said it was to "save" my career. Honestly! Could anyone truly think I—or anyone in television—would be so callous as to bring a life into this world to salvage a job in which they were miserable? As far as I was concerned, those stories were just the latest in a litany to which I'd grown accustomed.

And so when Niki was born, I suppose I shouldn't have been surprised—or hurt—when the one person who should have been closest to me on the program only off-handedly acknowledged his birth. I wasn't looking for a gift, but a card or phone call from Bryant might have been nice. What I got was a top-of-the-line e-mail message on the computer, something like, "Congrats on the new arrival."

I just stopped and reread this section.

I realize that what was going on was a gradual whittling away of my self-confidence. A chipping away at the person who had been Deborah Norville. I had become distrustful of the people I was supposed to look to for guidance. I felt isolated from the persons with whom I should have had the closest working relationship. The gal who used to crack a joke or have a smart-aleck aside on *Sunrise* had been relegated to a "speak when you are spoken to" role on *Today*.

You think I'm kidding! I wish I were. I was told never to initiate conversation on the program. But I was told that in a bit more direct fashion.

When Niki was born, I just wanted to escape. I was thrilled to have this beautiful *and healthy* little boy in my arms. I had had a difficult first pregnancy. At about thirty-two weeks' gestation, my blood pressure went sky high and I was diagnosed with toxemia, a potentially life-threatening condition. My obstetrician wanted me to take to my bed, but the Persian Gulf War had just begun. I couldn't leave *then!* Our compromise was that I would lie down on my left side, the least stressful for the baby, in between my segments on the program, which some days would run for six hours instead of two because of war updates.

Unfortunately, a convenient dressing room just outside the studio could not be made available to me. So I'd have to waddle a ways down the hall to a vacant room past the control room. I'm sure those viewers with eagle eyes wondered why I was a bit rumpled on one side.

I suspect the stress I was under played some role in my medical condition. I continue to thank God that Niki seemed to bear no ill effects of the unhappy professional situation that accompanied my pregnancy. Or maybe he does. He can be the grumpiest person in the world when he wakes up. Maybe that's his way of getting back at me for all those early morning disturbances in utero before he was born!

Niki's birth was such a joy for us. I'll never forget the moment he emerged into this world. There were huge windows in the delivery room. It was cloudy that day, but the moment Niki was born—3:24 P.M. on February 27—the clouds broke for a moment. The most incredibly bright sunshine came streaming into the delivery room. I can still see the rays of sunshine angling into the room. As a child, we thought the sun rays were how angels got to heaven. I knew my own little angel was being blessed by God.

Like any new parents we wanted to share our joy with the world. And when you work in television, you get the chance to share your good news with a wider audience. Naturally, when Alan Carter, then a reporter with *People* magazine, asked to do a story about our little guy, we were thrilled to say yes.

By this point, I wasn't about to ask "the experts" what they thought about the idea. In fact, Alan asked me why I hadn't wanted to do the maternity diary they'd asked about the previous autumn when I announced my pregnancy. I said, "What diary?"

Alan explained that the magazine had thought a day-by-day sharing of my thoughts of impending motherhood might be a good story. This was news to me: no one at NBC had ever told me. Alan said that after several weeks without an answer, he called the NBC News publicist for a response. Alan told me she said, "I guess she wasn't interested." I would have loved to compile such a diary. What a wonderful memory of such a terrific time in one's life—even if *People* never used it. Are you beginning to see a pattern emerging here with these experts?

Without the advice and counsel of the experts, Karl and I talked with Alan. The result was a lovely story, entitled "Today's Latest Coo." It was a nice mix of photos and comments from us about what we thought parenthood would be like. Niki was just days old when Harry Benson came to our house to take the pictures. He was there a long time and when it came time to feed the child, I fed him. Brother! What a ruckus that caused!

Niki was breast-fed those first few months and when I nursed Niki, Harry took a beautiful and very discreet photograph. It is one of my most cherished mementos of Niki's early days.

The way folks reacted, you'd have thought I had a staple in my navel. Suddenly I was the week's topic on talk radio across the country and (once again!) headline material for the papers. *Debo-*

rah Norville nursing in public! For crying out loud, I was sitting in my own home. As for the scandalous photo, well, I've got evening dresses that show more skin! The La Leche League even called asking me to become their spokeswoman.

To be honest with you, I was a little bit amused by all the hoopla. If nothing else, I figured, it was a good reminder to folks that the best thing you can do for your baby is to give him mother's milk if possible. No way they could make me a villain in this episode, right?

Guess again! One of the experts, an "NBC executive" as they were identified in a New York paper, said, "This will typecast Deborah in that motherhood role and be negative for her career."

Excuse me? Being in a magazine story about becoming a mother will typecast me? And being typecast as a *mother* is going to hurt my career? "These people are nuts," I told myself. And I knew then that I had to get out.

Realizing that I had to leave was really not that hard. After all, it had been a long time since anyone on the show had made me feel particularly wanted. There had been enough "accidental" computer messages dumped in my file to make me feel unloved. Here's an example: "By March, we've got a second host who can pull those spots off . . ." To send an e-mail, one must type a specific name. Someone wanted me to see that ugly message. And I guess that's what hurt the most about knowing I had to go: no one would be begging me to stay.

And they didn't.

Once I was gone from *Today,* the crisis hit. Suddenly I'd gone from "fastest rising star" to "damaged goods." It's a label you never want put on you in my business. It's a curse, a cloud that hovers over you—frightening away anyone who might have been interested in using your services as a broadcaster.

I was a villainess, a back-stabber, a conniver and schemer. All you had to do was read the clip file on me to know that. Who's going to hire someone when the first thing the newspaper writers are going to do is a computer search that spews out a stream of negative stories? And how was I to change their minds and convince them it was all unfair?

I tried to take some solace—and pride—in the fact that no one ever criticized my work. I was never accused of being unprepared, of not knowing the subjects I would have to talk about. I knew my delivery was smooth and my live interviews focused—they'd told me that. I wasn't "relaxed" on the air. Could you be relaxed when every time you turned around someone was shouting, "Incoming!" and you just waited for the next bomb to explode?

I tried to accept what *I* knew was a fact: I would never work in television again. I'd been in the business since I was nineteen—and now, at age thirty-two, it was time to start looking for a new career. It's odd, but I *still* get that tight feeling across my chest and find it's hard to breathe deep enough to get enough oxygen. Is that what the beginning of a panic attack feels like?

All those words of the Golden Girl came back to haunt me. I used to tell groups I'd be asked to speak to, particularly students, to "take the blinders off." I often admonished my listeners to "not focus so intently on a goal that they miss the opportunities that lie along the periphery." I would put my hands on either side of my eyes to block view of all but those people seated directly in front of me. I couldn't see the people on the sides. In the same way, when we focus so strongly on one goal, we can often miss the other opportunities along the way.

Well, I was trying to take the blinders off now. And all I could see was nothingness.

My other big pronouncement came back to haunt me too. It was: "Guard your reputation like a vase. Once it's damaged, once it's cracked, you can never make it whole again. You may repair the break, but that crack will always be visible." "Great!" I now told myself, *"you've* got a crack the size of the Grand Canyon in your reputation!" I knew that crack, the *Today* show negative rap, would always be there.

The more I focused on this, the deeper I sank. I had a beautiful baby and a wonderful husband. But I no longer had a career.

And I realized that career had meant more to me than I'd ever imagined.

The days became a blur. There was a maddening cadence to it all: feeding Niki every three hours, discussing the details of my departure from NBC with my agent, then hanging up the telephone in tears. Poor Karl. When he'd come home from the office, he must have hesitated to open the front door. God knows what kind of shape I would be in when he walked in! And—I knew that the postpartum rush of hormones wasn't helping any either.

None of it made any sense to me. I never came up with an answer any of the eight zillion times I asked, "What did *I* do to deserve all this? What good was there to come from all this pain and confusion?" The other big trauma in my life, my mom's death, was something for which I could find a purpose. She'd been fighting medical problems more than half of my life. While I could never understand why a woman as smart and vibrant as Momma was plagued with such health troubles, I saw a purpose in her death. She was no longer in pain. And that was a huge comfort to me and my sisters.

There was no such solace now for me.

I think for anyone who's gone through a crisis—and the more I talk about this subject, the more I discover women who have experienced the same kind of traumatic upheaval that I did—there comes a turning point, an epiphany, which marks the beginning of the end. Mine came when Niki was about three months old.

It had been another bad day. I never did get dressed. Never did take a shower. Probably hadn't brushed my hair. That was nothing unusual. Most days I did absolutely nothing for myself.

It was dinnertime and Karl and I had just sat down at the dining room table. Thank God for Eulon, our wonderful housekeeper, and Juliette, the nurse who was helping take care of the baby. If it hadn't been for them, there would have been many nights when Karl would have starved. Preparing meals was just another thing I wasn't doing.

One night Juliette had made a wonderful supper. She'd set the table using the good china and my mom's silver. It was a delicious meal of steamed rice, sauteed shrimp, and Caribbean style mixed vegetables. It looked wonderful. And I couldn't eat a bite. I couldn't lift my fork. All I could do was cry. I sat there, my spine practically curling onto itself. My posture was as low as my image of myself.

Poor Karl. He tried to make me feel better. He reminded me of how mean so many people at NBC had been. He pointed out all those people who'd said they would call—and never did. He reminded me of that beautiful little baby upstairs sleeping. None of it helped. I just sat there and cried. My head hung so low, it was practically in my plate.

That's when Karl took me by the hand and led me upstairs. He said, "Go to sleep. You're exhausted—just sleep until you wake up."

I protested, "But Niki. What about the baby? He has to be fed."

Karl was firm. "He'll be fine. I'll give him a bottle."

I relented. "Okay. But wake me when he needs to be fed."

"Sure, of course we will," Karl said, with absolutely no intention of waking me up.

So, I cried myself to sleep. And I slept. I slept for nearly twelve hours. It was the first real sleep I'd had in more than a year. Even before I'd become pregnant, I had had trouble sleeping. I know now that is just one of the signs of depression. I was almost always awake before the 3:30 A.M. alarm had gone off. My mind was always trying to figure out ways to make the nightmare at work get better.

So when I collapsed in sleep that day, it was the kind of peaceful, restful slumber that had eluded me for years.

And when I woke up—wow! Was I uncomfortable. Twelve hours without nursing the baby had left my breasts engorged and very painful. I got in the shower and tried to reduce the swelling— and again I cried. But this time, it was different. I cried and hated "them" for ruining what should have been one of the most joyful times in my life. I cried for the loss of my career. I cried about everything that had happened. But through my tears, I made myself a promise: I would never let "them" have this kind of impact on my personal life again.

Maybe I'd cared too much, I told myself.

Maybe it wasn't a moment as dramatic as when Scarlett made her pledge in the garden: "As God is my witness, I'll never be hungry again!" But there I was, my bloated body dripping wet in the shower—without the Technicolor, without the musical crescendo. I made my own pledge: "They'll never make me this miserable again!"

And when I got out of the shower, I got dressed. It was my first step toward getting my life back on track.

Chapter Two

FACING FACTS

"Women have the capacity in their hearts for sins they never committed."

—Cornelia Otis Skinner

If I had a penny for every minute I've spent trying to figure out what happened at NBC, I'd be living on easy street. "What did I do wrong?" I've asked myself a million times. "Who did I tick off? Which toes did I step on inadvertently?" I've wondered time and again.

I thought I was being a good girl. Doing all the right things, trying *not* to put myself in a situation where someone could say "Norville's reaching . . . better watch out for her!" Trust me, you spend any amount of time in the television news business and you will witness some astonishing feats of brownnosing.

Occasionally an industry function will mean you are in a social situation with your bosses—or the people you *wish* were your bosses. I always feel like a child at those things. Yet I have seen some incredible operators at work.

Yes—politics *is* a part of television news, though I've never actually heard of a situation in which one TV reporter was able to get another shipped to Alaska as did the ambitious climber in the movie *Broadcast News*. (However, that movie *was* true to life in that one scene in which the network executive from New York asked the aging correspondent he'd just fired if "there was anything he could do." The ex-employee replies, "Yes, you could die early." I have it on *good* authority that *did* happen at one of the network bureaus in Washington! But I digress . . .)

I racked my brain. I beat myself up about what happened at *Today,* knowing it *must* have been something I'd done. Then, the more I thought about it, the more I realized I have a tendency to assume responsibility for *everything* that goes wrong. Maybe it's a female thing. We all do it. I used to think it was just me. The curse of being a Type A personality.

But I was wrong. It's a genetic trait. It's something *all* women do. We women are magnets. Like the Charlie Brown character Pig Pen seems to attract dirt, there is something about women's personalities that encourages troubles to just glom onto us.

When I started talking about this out loud, did I get an earful in return. There are countless numbers of us females out there who feel a tremendous obligation to control everything in our lives—and, to be honest, everything else around us too.

I'm sure you've been to the card shop and seen those cute little pillows they march out every May just before Mother's Day: "God couldn't be everywhere, so he created mothers." It's a dear "aw shucks" sort of sentiment that makes us get a little teary and think about all the nice things our moms did for us.

Well, I've got a P.S., 1990s-style, addition to that:

. . . And mothers can't do everything so God created GUILT!

I now know how my own mother felt when I was four years old and was sent on the kindergarten class pony ride field trip without a sandwich. I was the only kid there without a lunch. Fortunately the teachers had prepared for the possibility that frazzled moms with four kids like my mother might forget about the sustenance of one of their brood. They'd brought extras. It was the first time I'd ever eaten peanut butter and jelly. (Does the fact that thirty plus years later I *still* remember this indicate that this event had an impact on me?)

And I can now appreciate how *guilt-filled* Mom must have felt that day. I was headed in that direction even before I had kids.

I remember when the women and guilt association became clear to me: it was a few years ago. I'm very lucky in that I have a housekeeper who, among other things, helps with the laundry. So why is it I felt *guilty* when my husband called from the bedroom one morning, "Deb, where are my black socks?"

"In your drawer," I replied, "right where I put them."

"No . . ." Karl disagreed. "There are no black socks in here. They're all blue."

Now I know that I had just recently bought him four brand-new pairs of black socks at Bloomingdale's. Took the tags off, stuck them in his drawer. So I went to look for myself.

He was right. There was not a single pair of black socks in there. Somehow they'd all turned blue in the wash.

Socks are not my department. I had not laid a finger on those socks since I bought them. Yet here I was feeling responsible for the fact that they had been transformed into a new hue.

And it truly pained me. No wonder a quarter of us women are mildly depressed at any given time. If a pair of socks can set you off . . . Heavens, a real problem very well might do me in!

I don't think I'm all that unusual.

I've found that a lot of us women have an almost innate reaction that gives us ownership over the dynamics of a situation.

It's the "if only" routine. "If only" I'd gotten there sooner. "If only" I'd made one more phone call. "If only" I'd gotten up earlier.

They say emotion comes very easily to women. But it's not the "cry at the drop of a hat" kind of emotion. It's guilt. Look again at that quote from Cornelia Otis Skinner. Why is it women are inclined to feel responsible for everything? Are we inherently meddlers? Or is it something deeper?

Call it egotism, but I think a great many of us believe as women that "if only" we'd been involved, the situation would have gone differently (better, of course—after all, *we* would have been calling the shots). The fact that we weren't involved in this less-than-perfect situation is something that pains us mightily. It's an outgrowth of the reality that most women wear a number of different hats.

Think for a moment of the many responsibilities that are primarily yours. At home, you may be a wife and mother, which typically means you are in charge of planning meals, the family's social life, cooking and cleaning—or seeing that it gets done—household repairs, children's doctor and dental appointments, buying new shoes and clothes when the old ones are outgrown, and getting kids to school and back and to all the extracurricular activities. And that's just at home!

Add to that your involvement with your church, synagogue, or other place of worship, volunteer work you may do, and a full- or part-time job and it's easy to see why we women think we can do it all: we're asked to on a daily basis.

Consequently, when some little something *doesn't* go according to plan, we accept responsibility for the failure, even when the fault may well rest somewhere else.

Men, you may have noticed, don't do that.

Look at what happens when a man meets a setback. He acts—or reacts. When trouble strikes, he may get drunk. He may call his buddies and play a four-hour game of full-contact basketball. He may hit. When the male of the species meets with failure, he gets physical.

What do we do?

We think about it. We sit down and ask ourselves, "What did I do wrong? What could I have done differently?" We analyze the situation to within an inch of its life. And the more we think about it, because of our innate tendency to assume responsibility for everything around us ("I am woman, hear me roar!"), the more down in the dumps we get. And this is just when *little* things go wrong. Imagine what happens when the bottom falls out of our lives.

No wonder women outnumber men two to one in suffering depression.

• • •

"I knew how to act appropriate and act sane and act okay and that's exactly what I did. It was acting. Inside there was this emptiness. There was no emotional core."

Joan Esposito is not the kind of woman one can ever picture struggling with depression. She is one of those born gorgeous women with the sort of striking beauty that forces people to draw an involuntary gasp upon first meeting her. She's got a great figure that she amazingly doesn't seem to have to work at to keep and jet black hair. Her face is punctuated by brown eyes that are so sharp and so focused they almost compel you to look into them. And on top of all that, she's incredibly nice!

Yet what is most noticeable about Joan is the clarity and recall with which she speaks about the day she would give anything to forget.

"I remember standing over him and screaming. Saying over and over again the same thing: 'Nothing can be this bad! *Nothing* can be this bad!' Like I could reason with him!" There is a weariness in Joan's voice as she relives the day her world changed forever.

It was January 31, 1993. It was the kind of frigid winter day when the wind off the lake could cut through as many layers of clothes as you put on. Joan's husband, Bryan Harwood, had come to their cottage on Lake Michigan to think. That in and of itself wasn't unusual. He was an artist and when he needed inspiration— or when he and Joan had had an argument—he often came to this oasis away from the hectic pace of Chicago to get away.

This time it was an argument that brought Bryan to the house over the weekend. And as was the case every other time he'd gone to the lake house to think, Bryan had left a message on Joan's voice mail at work saying he loved her.

"I felt really great getting that," Joan relates, "because I knew how Bryan's moods went. When I got the 'I love you' message, I knew in a few hours I would get the follow-up message. He would apologize for picking the fight."

But the follow-up message never came.

After three days of alternately being pleased that Bryan was taking some time for himself and berating him for not calling, Joan finally got up early and drove to her Michigan cottage. "I thought I'll check on him. I'll yell at him for not calling, and then I'll go back to work."

Instead, the moment she walked into the house Joan sensed something was terribly wrong. A huge painting on one wall of the living room had been repainted—with a frightening message of finality.

"The first thing that went into my mind was 'This reads like a suicide note. . . .' And then I thought, 'No, it can't be—don't be so *dramatic!* '"

Hesitantly, Joan took another step into the living room, toward the windows that looked out toward the lake. It was a view she and Bryan had spent many hours sharing together. The sight would haunt Joan for the rest of her life.

"I saw his body outside. I think he had been dead two or three days by the time I found him. He was frozen solid. Absolutely frozen solid." As Joan speaks, you can tell she's drifting back to that day that, no matter how much she tries, she can't erase from her memory.

"It was really rather ingenious," she laughs with no small amount of irony in her voice. "This was no spur-of-the-moment action. He'd taken a shotgun and tied a string to the trigger and then tied the string around his foot so that with his hands he could hold the barrel in his mouth."

When Joan discovered her husband's body, she rushed outside, but there was nothing she could do. Bryan's decision to end his life had changed hers as well. She stood helplessly screaming in the snow. She said later, "I'd always thought it was writer's hyperbole when they described screams being ripped from your body. But that's what it was. It was as though a huge fist were reaching inside and pulling the screams out of my body. It was amazingly horrific."

It was there in the snow that Joan made what she later realized would be the first of many truly life-and-death decisions. In the midst of her screams, she was very consciously aware of a still, quiet place inside her mind. It was an oasis. A place of peace. And it beckoned with a seductiveness that in her moment of crisis Joan was barely able to resist.

"I was very drawn to that place," she recalls softly. "It was a little calm spot and it had a siren song. But there was a part of me that knew that if I went there, I would never come back. Even in that weakened state, I *knew* that quiet place represented catatonia and complete disconnection from the world.

"I had a choice. I could stay with the conscious woman who was hurting incredibly and screaming or I could go to the quiet place where it was going to be very safe and protected. But it was a place I would never leave.

"At that moment I made a choice to stay alive and experience the pain knowing, intellectually at least, that one day it would subside."

As Joan sits in her office and quietly describes the day she discovered her husband's body, it is impossible not to marvel at her calm as she talks. She is not exactly detached, but there is a placidness or maybe a resignation to her speech.

Perhaps that is a reflection of Joan's professional life. She is one of Chicago's best known and most respected television anchorwomen. News of the sudden death of her husband—and the circumstances in which he died—spread faster through the Windy City than the Great Chicago Fire. The rumor mills were soon running at top speed.

That's because just days before Bryan's suicide, Joan had discovered she was expecting. It had been only ten months earlier that Karl and I had been with Joan and Bryan celebrating their marriage. It was a glorious day. And Joan and Bryan both looked completely radiant. She had worn a magnificent ecru silk gown and had woven strands of pearls through her hair. It had reminded me of the way I imagined mermaids must do their coiffures. Joan and Bryan said their I do's on the roof of her brand-new townhouse—which he had helped her build.

Joan is one of the few people whose construction project

wasn't a nightmare. I remember joking with her when she started dating Bryan. "That's a sneaky way to get your house finished! Go out with your builder!" We'd both laughed. In our long-distance phone visits, I could tell that Bryan was someone with whom Joan felt comfortable and who made her happy. And though he was a quiet man, it seemed to me, anyway, that he'd adjusted well to the baggage that goes along with dating a popular television personality like Joan.

Like they say, appearances can be deceiving.

I was on assignment for CBS in San Francisco when a friend called me with the news of Bryan's death. I remember rushing to Joan's house as soon as I could break free of the shoot. And I'll never forget holding Joan when I arrived and her whisper through our hug, "Deb—I'm pregnant."

In that moment, I recall nearly drowning in a flood of emotions: sadness for the baby who wouldn't have a father, loneliness for Joan, who would be traveling the path to parenthood alone, and regret that after a string of lousy relationships and bad boyfriends, once again my friend was being robbed. It was so un*fair!*

But for Joan, it got worse. Sometimes, when I think I just can't handle another thing that God might send my way, I think of Joan. Talk about made of steel!

Since Bryan Harwood's death was a suicide, it wasn't widely reported on the news. Generally the media don't report suicides unless the decedent is a public figure. But while the papers didn't report his death, that didn't stop people from gossiping about it.

For a while Joan's friends were able to shield her from the worst of it. But eventually Joan heard the rumors—*after* they had been broadcast on the CBS-owned FM radio station in town.

"They went on the air and said I caused his suicide. A few days later they asked their listeners to call in and give their opinion as to whether or not I should abort the baby. And then, a week or two after that was when they went on the air and said an anchorwoman is pregnant with a Chicago Bulls player's baby. I was the only anchorwoman pregnant at the time."

Today Joan recites the litany of offensive comments as though she were reading her grocery list. But at the time, the injustice of the remarks and the cruelty behind them were incapacitating.

On top of that, she felt her job was in jeopardy. While officials at her television station were solicitous, they also soon pressed Joan to "give us an idea" of when she might return to the anchor desk. She was back on the job two weeks after Bryan's death.

"Oddly enough, it was probably the most therapeutic thing I could do. When you anchor you have to at least reasonably concentrate on what you're doing. So for at least thirty minutes a day, I was guaranteed I wouldn't think about it. It was the only thirty minutes in the day when I did *not* think about Bryan.

The rest of the time, Joan was constantly reliving that moment of finding Bryan's body and tormenting herself with the unanswerable question—"Why?" As she put it: "I was simply paralyzed."

That was quite a change from the woman who used to feel that anything that landed on her plate, she could handle. And when she'd compare the way she felt about herself with an unborn baby and an uncertain future as opposed to her old can-do, accomplish-anything self—it made her even more blue.

IT TAKES BOTH RAIN AND SUNSHINE TO MAKE A RAINBOW

Joan's crisis was obvious and understandable. But sometimes, it is difficult for many of us to recognize how far we've fallen because we are so far down in a hole. When a person is depressed, it changes everything about their world. You think differently. The way you look at life around you, your impression about yourself, your sense of the future—all become bleak.

The good times in life are behind you. Small obstacles are major, insurmountable impediments. When I was at my lowest point, I was defeated by a box. A package had arrived and the scissors were upstairs. Rather than take the box upstairs with me—or head up to bring the scissors down to the box—the box simply remained sealed. It was just too hard to take the few steps necessary to get what I needed to open the box.

When you are defeated, you analyze every situation that hasn't worked out in your life and you *know* you are the reason for the failure. You are alone because you are not worthy of having companionship. You lost your job because your performance was bad. Your child became ill because you weren't attentive enough as a mom. When you analyze the reasons for your setback, they all point in one direction: to you. And you know, because the problem is *you,* nothing will ever change.

If these words come close to describing the way *you* feel, as the old saying goes, misery loves company, so you should be feeling pretty good. When you look at depression statistics, the numbers are on the upswing.

Over the course of the last seventy years, the rate of Americans whose outlook has sunk to the depths has increased steadily. When the U.S. government studied depression rates in more than 9,500 people, the results were startling: people born in the second half of this century are *ten times* more likely to suffer depression than those born in the first half of the twentieth century.

It's exactly the opposite of what one would expect. One would think that as one ages and experiences more downturns in life, their likelihood for depression would seem greater. You would expect as technology has made our lives easier (when is the last time you beat a rug outside?) and changing attitudes have opened more opportunities for employment and lifestyle choices, people would be more content.

Apparently progress has only complicated our lives. Researchers have found that persons born in 1925 had only a 4 percent rate of depression, while those born before the First World War had only a 1 percent depression rate.

According to the research, the later one is born, the greater the likelihood of depression. One study by the Oregon Research Institute compared depression episodes in adolescents. Of the kids born from 1968 to 1971, 4.5 percent had at least one bout with depression by age fourteen. But the younger kids, those born in 1972,

1973, and 1974, had nearly double the experience with depression. Of these, 7.2 percent had at least one episode of depression by the time they hit fourteen.

The experts will argue over the reasons. But the studies seem to point to our increasingly complicated, fast-paced world as, at the very least, conducive to those bouts of the blues.

Columnist Anna Quindlen once talked about the loss of old familiar guideposts. It used to be, she said, if you were Roman Catholic, you didn't use birth control. If you were a union member, you voted Democrat, and if you were a woman you stayed home with the kids. Do any of those old rules still apply?

In the 1970s we were introduced to "Superwoman"—the gal who could do everything. Frankly, I think we're still paying the price for *that* introduction.

Remember the old Enjoli perfume commercial of the 1970s?

> *I can bring home the bacon . . .*
> *Fry it up in a pan . . .*
> *And never let him forget he's a man . . .*
> *'Cause I'm a wo-o-o-man!*

Someone shoot her!

As Quindlen indicates, we definitely have many more choices today as women—but *choosing* among them hasn't gotten any easier. We can be anything we want to be—but *what,* we ask, is it we *want?* When you're already struggling with a faltering self-image, indecisiveness *certainly* doesn't help!

At any given time, 25 percent of the American population is undergoing some sort of depression. And 80 percent of those people are women. That is an astonishing figure. Think of it this way: of the kids in your carpool group, odds are at least *one* of their moms is struggling. And chances are . . . they would never admit it.

IF IT QUACKS LIKE A DUCK

I know during *my* dark times "depression" was the last label I wanted to assume. The labels I'd already given myself were heavy enough baggage: fat, unemployed, damaged goods. To call myself depressed would probably have been the nudge that would push me over the edge. What I didn't know was that I had gone over the edge a long time ago.

"I was a bad wife. I was a bad woman. I was a failure as a lover."
Robin's image of herself when her husband of thirteen years walked out used every negative image in the book. To an outsider looking in, she would be described as vivacious, energetic, trim, and engaging. The only positive thing Robin could say about herself was "I am an excellent mother."

The product of an abusive home, Robin had chosen for herself a mate who possessed all of the caring, empathetic qualities her own father did not. The shock of Don's leaving—there was no other woman; he just "wasn't happy" he said—incapacitated her. In the first days after the split, Robin found herself in bed, curled in the fetal position.

"It was just this mourning, where this crying would come out and it's sort of like a keening and a wailing. It's like a death, only worse because he didn't die. He just kept coming back [to see their two children] to remind me he was gone."

Robin was sinking deeper and deeper into despair.

"Life's but a walking shadow, a poor player
That struts and frets his hour upon the stage
And then is heard no more."

—Macbeth, in *Macbeth,* by William Shakespeare

When a person is depressed, the first change is in one's perception of *self*. Your weaknesses and faults become glaringly obvious and take on a new (and unrealistic) importance. Because your own inadequacies (real and imagined) have assumed Herculean proportions, you become convinced that everything you attempt will be a failure. After all, *you* are a failure, why shouldn't everything you touch fail as well?

From a negative sense of self, one digresses into a negative change in *mood*. You may become sad and weepy. You may become anxious or angry. I remember watching television with little Niki in my arms and just sobbing uncontrollably when I saw the plight of the Kurds, who were then being bombed by Iraq. It was natural to be moved by the fate of these people—it was unnatural to react so physically to it.

It's possible you might move on to become numb and unfeeling—unresponsive to the world. You walk zombielike through the routine of daily life, able to act only because you are moving through the rut of getting up, going to work, coming home. Life is just a series of days strung together.

The next symptom of depression is a change in *behavior*. Indecision becomes the byword in your life. When faced with even the simplest decision—should we eat chicken or fish—you become paralyzed. The most routine of daily chores seems challenging. Remember me and the box? And at the first sign of difficulty, you find it preferable to give up instead of meeting the challenge.

Finally, the changes become *physical*. You can't eat, or eating is the only thing that satisfies you. You can't sleep and get up in the middle of the night to tidy the house. Your waking hours are spent wishing for the sleep that eluded you the night before. Or you might find your bed is the only safe place in the world, and getting out of it some days is simply impossible.

When the *Today* show nightmare was going on, no one in New York City had better organized cupboards than I. Even though I had to wake up at four o'clock every morning to get ready for work, I usually got up long before that. I would toss and turn in bed for a couple of hours, watching the red glow of the alarm clock as it flipped minute upon minute . . . eventually watching the hours go by. I could precisely predict when the digital clock was going to switch from 2:37 A.M. to 2:38 A.M.

Since I was up anyway, I figured I may as well be useful. So I'd pull on my robe and pad downstairs to the kitchen where I would take all the canned goods out and the cake mixes and the cookies and cereal. Then I'd wash down the shelves and replace everything. I took great pleasure in discovering the right combination of cans to stack on top of one another. Sometimes, I would take the gravy mixes and alphabetize them. If there were two open boxes of grits or cornmeal, I'd consolidate them into one container.

This nocturnal activity would make me very happy. I might not feel much accomplishment about the situation at the office, but boy oh boy, those neat and clean cupboards were really something!

At the time, I never could understand why Karl didn't share my pleasure with my kitchen work.

As you can see from the chart below, depression is a progression. You might not find you've taken all of the steps, but the more these *do* describe you—and the more severely you experience them—the more likely you are to be suffering some form of depression.

Stages of Depression

1. Negative view of yourself
2. Your mood becomes negative
3. Negative changes in behavior
4. Significant physical changes

Do any of these apply to you? Maybe it's time for you to take the first step toward getting your life back on track.

STEP ONE TO GETTING BACK ON TRACK: ACKNOWLEDGE YOU'RE HAVING A CRISIS

Alcoholics Anonymous has helped millions of people successfully beat drinking problems. While the paths of their journeys to recovery may have taken different routes, each began the same way: by acknowledging a problem. "My name is Bill. I'm an alcoholic."

Take a look at this questionnaire prepared by the American Psychiatric Association. If you answer yes to five or more of these questions and if the symptoms described have been present nearly every day for at least two weeks, maybe it's time you owned up to the impact the crisis has had on your life. Maybe it's time to *get your life back*.

Yes   No

—— —— 1. Do you feel a deep sense of depression, sadness, or hopelessness most of the day?

—— —— 2. Have you experienced diminished interest in most or all activities?

—— —— 3. Have you experienced significant appetite or weight change when not dieting?

—— —— 4. Have you experienced a significant change in sleeping patterns?

—— —— 5. Do you feel unusually restless . . . or unusually sluggish?

—— —— 6. Do you feel unduly fatigued?

—— —— 7. Do you experience persistent feelings of hopelessness or inappropriate feelings of guilt?

—— —— 8. Have you experienced a diminished ability to think or concentrate?

—— —— 9. Do you have recurrent thoughts of death or suicide?

My own recovery from my crisis didn't start by answering affirmatively to this questionnaire (I hadn't seen this at that time). I didn't join a group, didn't proclaim to the masses that I had a problem—I simply quietly admitted to myself, "Living like this is no fun; I've lost my sense of self and somehow I've got to get out of this funk."

I knew what the stakes were. On the surface, I was the woman who had it all: nice apartment on Park Avenue, handsome husband, a healthy baby. I was famous and financially comfortable.

The real picture was much more gloomy: I barely talked to my husband, except to cry. I sat all day long in the same saggy spot on the sofa—either glued to the television and tormenting myself that I wasn't working or glumly staring at the blank screen.

And while Karl was a prince during all the tough times, I knew that at some point his patience would wear out. Who wants to come home to a woman who is the personification of negative? Rather than take the baby's cries of discomfort or hunger in stride (the way I have with my second son), Niki's wailing would set me off . . . there I was, crying again.

That day at the dining room table, that night I was so filled with regret and remorse over the way my dream job had turned out, the time I couldn't bring myself to perform the most maternal of acts and nurse my baby—I knew I was depressed. I knew the old Debbie Norville was gone. And I resolved to find her again.

For me to get back on track, it took hitting bottom. It required that I consciously acknowledge that I'd lost control of my life. I had to recognize that this formerly Type A person who seemed so together had been turned into a little boat floating on the water without a rudder. I had to admit that I was simply being buffeted by the waves. Unless I made some changes, I knew my little boat would wash ashore somewhere I didn't want to be.

Maybe you can't bring yourself to say, "I am depressed." I know I couldn't. But before you can get better, before you can regain control of your life, you have to admit you don't have control. Before you can like yourself, you have to evaluate yourself honestly and be able to say, "I don't like who I've become."

• • •

*"I overheard my daughter one Saturday about 5:30 in the after-
noon telling one of her friends on the phone, 'No, I don't want to go
out tonight because I don't want to leave Mom alone.' And I thought
to myself, 'What have I done to her? She's young. She's giving up her
whole life to stay here with me night and day.'"*

It took an overheard telephone conversation for Ruth Brody to
realize how dependent she'd become on her twenty-five-year-old
daughter during her recovery from breast cancer. "I was depending
on her for everything, for every decision. And every time I cried, I
needed her to be there to give me a hug. I couldn't do anything
alone."

For fifty-one-year-old Ruth Brody, the last several years are
marked, not by family events like weddings and births, but by op-
erations. It started in mid-May of 1989 when she was diagnosed
with breast cancer. It's a devastating diagnosis for any woman, but
given Ruth's family history, to her it was a death sentence. Her sister, her mother, her grandfather, her uncle, and her sister-in-law all
died of cancer.

The day she got the news, she just went home and cried. "It
was the end of my life. Everyone I ever knew with cancer died
within a year or two years, so consequently when I was diagnosed,
I figured the same was going to happen to me. I was devastated. I
started preparing my will, and somewhere in my mind I conjured
up that I had one year to live."

Ruth brought the same businesslike efficiency to her cancer
that she used running her import business. When a routine mam-
mogram detected a suspicious mass that was later confirmed to be
cancerous, Ruth quickly got the opinions of five different doctors
and within two weeks she underwent a mastectomy and immediate reconstruction.

That was only the beginning.

What physical stamina she didn't lose through an aggressive
program of chemotherapy was sapped through a succession of
surgeries. Three months after her mastectomy, there was a problem

with Ruth's interim implant that required an operation. In October, she underwent an in-office gynecologic procedure. Then a hysterectomy in December. The permanent implant went in in February. That didn't work so it was replaced in April. And when that one was unsuccessful, Ruth had yet a third permanent implant surgery (by a new doctor!) in November.

With so many medical problems to contend with, Ruth couldn't cope with the stress of running a business. So she closed her company and soon she found herself facing a myriad of medical bills without affordable private insurance to cover them.

"I just went deeper and deeper and deeper. I just had so many losses that I felt even if I lived, I could never get a handle on my life again."

In the professional world, "depressed" is a medical term. I do not use the word in the clinical sense, but rather in the way most people have adopted it to describe the malaise and lack of purpose that so many of us feel from time to time in our lives.

> I am now the most miserable man living. If what I feel were equally distributed to the whole human family, there would not be one cheerful face on earth. Whether I shall ever be better, I cannot tell; I am awfully forebode I shall not. To remain as I am is impossible. I must die or be better, it appears to me.

Pretty depressing reading, isn't it? It was written by Abraham Lincoln in 1841 about three weeks after breaking off his engagement to Mary Todd.

It's not easy to say, "I'm depressed." Sometimes it's better to let the evidence speak for itself. While there is no way to predict with certainty a person's likelihood to become depressed, there are a few criteria that can let you know if you're headed in that direction.

First of all, your history. If you have had a depressive episode in the past, you're at greater risk to become depressed again. The *Journal of Clinical Psychiatry* reports that half of the people who've had a major depression will have a recurrence within two or three years. Life events can also help as a predictor.

Take a look at this Stress Scale, put together by researchers at the University of Washington School of Medicine. Though this list was first drafted thirty years ago, it is still a useful indicator. If any of these things have happened to you in the past twelve months, jot down the point score and continue on down the list.

Death of spouse	100
Divorce	73
Marital separation	65
Jail term	63
Death of close family member	63
Personal injury or illness	53
Marriage	50
Fired from job	47
Marital reconciliation	45
Retirement	45
Change in family member's health	44
Pregnancy	40
Sex difficulties	39
Addition to family	39
Business readjustment	39
Change in financial status	38
Death of close friend	37
Change to different line of work	36
Change in number of marital arguments	36
Mortgage or loan over $10,000	31
Foreclosure of loan or mortgage	30
Change in work responsibilities	29
Son or daughter leaving home	29
Trouble with in-laws	29
Outstanding personal achievement	28
Spouse begins or stops work	26
Starting or finishing school	26
Change in living conditions	25

Revision of personal habits	24
Trouble with boss	23
Change in work hours, conditions	20
Change in residence	20
Change in schools	20
Change in recreational habits	19
Change in church activities	19
Mortgage or loan under $10,000	17

Remember this list was compiled over thirty years ago. There are a number of stresses in the 1990s that I would add to the list, including fertility troubles, substance abuse, and commuting to work as well as Christmas and family vacations.

If your score is over 300, you are supposedly at 80 percent risk for depression or stress-related illness. Those scoring between 200 and 300 are said to have a 50 percent risk. When I took the test, I realized that for me, the question was not, "Was I depressed?" But rather, "Would I ever muddle my way out of it?"

Being able to admit to yourself that you are depressed, or not happy, or have lost control—whatever form your moment of truth takes—is not easy. But remember this, once you've hit bottom, there's only one way to go. Once you've taken the first step toward getting better—that first act that will ultimately result in you getting back on track—the next steps won't be nearly as hard.

I found it was wonderfully empowering, even before I'd begun to get my sense of self-esteem back, to be able to say, "Professionally speaking, life will never be as tough as it had been." There was *no one* who could argue that point with me.

What were the odds that my career could again blow up in my face and on the tube the way it had? You know the old saying, "Fool me once, shame on you. Fool me twice, shame on *me!*" While I couldn't predict the course of my personal life and what pitfalls might lay ahead, I was fairly confident that what had happened to me at *Today* would never happen again.

Perhaps for you, admitting that you've hit your own bottom isn't so difficult. It may be that you find it difficult to believe that you'll ever be able to feel that you are back on track. You may think you'll never feel good about yourself again. I promise, you can. "Easy for you to say, Deborah," you think to yourself. "You've got this great job on TV and all that! *My* life's never going to come together again."

Honey, that is exactly the way I felt too! It's a long road you will travel—and where you are headed is someplace new. You are not trying to get back to the old you. The old you was defeated by crisis. The old you couldn't handle the surprises.

As I said, "depression" is also used as a clinical term. Severely clinically depressed people most likely can benefit from professional help. If you think this applies to you or someone you know, please refer to the Resources section in the back of this book for some organizations you can call upon.

Chances are, though, you won't call that professional. I know it's the *last* thing I would have done. I recently spoke to a group of career women in North Carolina. They were gathered for a day of seminars on networking, time management, organization of meetings, and so forth. They were heavy hitters on the fast track with their careers.

Of the women who were kind enough to complete a little survey I passed around, 100 percent said they had experienced a life crisis. And yet less than one quarter of them sought professional help to resolve their situation. And 99.4 percent of the women reported that *they* had helped get themselves out of their bad situations.

Depending upon your crisis, you may have a lot to let go of. Lynn's husband walked out on her. Mentally she was constantly sticking pins in the imaginary voodoo doll of her spouse and envisioning all sorts of horrible things for him. But that wasn't doing a thing toward helping her get on with her life. Pat was downsized out of a job. Her despair over her corporate loyalty not being returned kept her from marshaling her energies toward finding that new and better position.

Today these women and thousands like them are enjoying a life of fulfillment and joy. They are back on track. Like every woman in North Carolina who shared with me, they feel *better* about themselves now than they ever did. Each of their journeys began with a silent confession to themselves: I need help.

Chapter Three

STEP BY STEP

"The journey of one thousand miles begins with a single step."

—Chinese proverb

WE'RE GOING THROUGH A WONDERFUL stage at our house. Kyle's learning to walk. Any day now, he's going to let go of that chair or coffee table and he's going to take off. And look out world when he does!

Right now, he's in what I call the "wounded duck walk" stage. When he's got someplace he needs to get to quickly, he drops to all fours and starts his own special version of the crawl. Hands are flying, one knee is propelling him forward, and on the other side, his foot is on the floor shoving him along. It may not be pretty, but it gets him where he wants to go.

My prescription for getting back on track is sort of the same. Just as no "Baby Handbook of Walking" would recommend the wounded duck walk method of locomotion, the experts probably would laugh at my way to get back on track. Which is probably a great endorsement! Any day now, Kyle's going to take that first step. But he's been working toward it for a long time. He's been strengthening his thigh muscles by pulling up on things. He's been improving his balance by briefly letting go and then quickly grabbing back again. He'll stand up for just a moment—and then plop right down on his bottom. It's not that stay-dry lining that he likes in his Pampers, but the extra padding on the bottom.

Working toward the new you is much the same. Just as Kyle's journey toward the world of the walking has been a process of small, seemingly insignificant stages, your journey will be the same.

A TURTLE ONLY MOVES FORWARD WHEN HE STICKS HIS NECK OUT

Have you ever watched a turtle? With a five-year-old boy, we're constantly on the lookout for interesting wildlife, and every so often we'll see a turtle plodding alongside the road. One time, Niki and I stopped and brought the turtle home to watch him in our yard for a while.

As you'd expect, Mr. Turtle (or Ms. Turtle, I'm not really sure how you tell the difference!) initially withdrew his head and feet and enclosed himself in his hard shell. But a few moments after we set him on the ground, he must have figured the coast was clear.

First his feet emerged, then, very slowly, his head peeked out. As the turtle got his bearings, Niki marveled at the reptile's intricate claws, his skinny tail, and the extra skin that seemed to hang like an elephant's around his neck.

Then the turtle stuck his neck out a bit further and took a step. Then his head bobbed back and came forward again and he took another step. And so forth.

And I said to Niki, "Look, Niki, the turtle only goes forward if his head comes out!"

And as we sat in the yard and watched the turtle slowly and methodically head toward the woods—and freedom—I found myself reflecting on what I'd just said to Niki. "The turtle only goes forward if his head comes out." If he doesn't stick his neck out, he's not going anywhere.

And so it is in life.

When you're hurting, when you feel overwhelmed by events that have taken place, it's very difficult to imagine putting yourself even more at risk. It's real hard to imagine sticking your neck out.

But think of that poor turtle.

He had every reason to expect that crazy lady and that boy are going to pick him up again and turn him over and poke at his tail and tickle his feet. The safe thing to do would have been to sit right there in his shell with the doors closed until he *knew* it was safe to move along. Wait it out. Let the world spin on by for a very long time . . . and then . . . maybe, see about moving along.

But he didn't. He stuck out his neck and took a step. And when the lady and the boy didn't grab him, he took another step and then another.

And before he knew it—and before we could say "Goodbye, Mr. Turtle"—he had disappeared into the woods.

Did that turtle set for himself the goal of hightailing it to the woods? I doubt it. Of course, I don't know that goal setting is something that turtles are known for—we'll have to consult the reptile experts on that one.

No, I suspect the turtle told himself, "Let's take a step and see what happens." His goal was small and insignificant.

That's the second step in getting back on track. It's easy when you are resolving to come back from disaster to set lofty goals for yourself. Don't. Save the big goals for later. You can save the world in due course. For now, just aim for getting out of bed.

STEP TWO TOWARD GETTING BACK ON TRACK: TAKE BABY STEPS

Set tiny little goals for yourself. Aim for things that are so laughably insignificant you are embarrassed to admit you've set them as a goal. You don't have to tell anyone your goals. Remember, your journey back from your crisis is, for now, a private one. You admitted to yourself—and yourself alone—that you've hit bottom; you can get a little help from your friends later.

For now, aim low. Take a step—*then* head for the woods.

I hope you won't laugh when you hear this: my first goal after my moment of truth in the shower was to get dressed in the morning. There would be days, even weeks sometimes, when I would stay in my nightgown and robe all day long.

But after that day when I decided I wasn't going to let them affect my life the way they had been, I resolved to make a big change. From that day forward, I would get dressed. "Nothing fancy—just put on clothes," I told myself.

Some days, it went well. I'd feed the baby at six in the morning, have breakfast with Karl before he left for work, and then get a quick shower before Niki woke up again, *and*—get dressed.

But it wasn't a steady progression. There were plenty of days when that bathrobe got a full day's workout.

Just because you *resolve* to change doesn't mean that you will. How many resolutions made at New Year's are history by Valentine's Day? Remember: all that's changed is your mind-set. The situation that brought you to your low point still exists. While you've resolved to achieve tiny goals, the big problem that's made your life so complicated still exists. But you're not strong enough to confront *that* demon. Not *yet* anyway.

Keep your steps tiny and your pace slow. I still cringe when I think of an accident that happened after Niki began walking. He and I were taking a stroll in the neighborhood on the day he turned two. He had managed to get just far enough ahead of me that I couldn't grab on to him.

He was walking just a bit too quickly and—you guessed it—

he fell. Like most toddlers, he didn't attempt to break his fall with his hands. Instead, he did a face plant in the street and broke his front tooth. It was a baby tooth and the dentist bonded it to protect it. But still, every time I look at that tooth and remember that fall, I cringe.

"If only" I'd been closer to Niki. "If only" I'd made him slow down. It's been a constant reminder to me that the old adage "slow and steady wins the race" really are words of wisdom.

When Ruth Brody was forced to face just how dependent she'd become on one of her daughters, Beth, who was living at home at the time, she realized she had to stop being a breast cancer victim and start being a survivor.

"I knew I had to pick it up and go on," Ruth explains. "Nobody was going to do this for me—no matter how many nights she was there with me. Nobody was going to turn my life around but *me.*"

Ruth described what she did next as "taking a little baby step." "My first baby step was to seek out a support system other than Beth."

Ruth started attending a breast cancer support group she'd heard of in the Chicago area called Y-Me? Her previous experiences with self-help groups had been profoundly disappointing, so she didn't expect much. She was shocked at the group of women she encountered.

"I saw these women who were so darned positive, and I thought, 'How can they be so positive?' And I knew I had to get rid of that self-pity and the energy I wasted feeling sorry for myself." Ruth says she started to spend a bit more time with some of the women she met. She'd occasionally join them for a cup of coffee after the meetings. In time, she noticed a big change of heart.

"I started to look forward to those things," she explains. "And I reached this point, I don't remember just when it was, but I reached this point where I thought, 'I'm *not* going to die. If they can live, *I* can live.'" Ruth sounds almost evangelical she is so enthusiastic as she shares her story. "And I started to think positively and anytime I got depressed, I would just push it out of my mind and get involved in something else."

It was at this point that Ruth let her many friends and the special man in her life be there for her. "He and I had gone our separate ways," she explains. "But when I was diagnosed with breast cancer, he was devastated and he came back. He said, 'I want to help you get through this.'

"And, I finally allowed myself to lean on my friends," Ruth remembers. For a woman who was fiercely independent, this was a big step. "They were extremely supportive and my network of friends were there for me whenever I needed them."

From that first support group meeting, Ruth has now become a director of the Y-Me organization, chairs their biggest fund-raiser, which draws more than two thousand attendees, and is lobbying the State of Illinois to change health insurance regulations so others won't have the struggle she did. That's quite a leap from the woman who updated her will after receiving her diagnosis!

It all started with one tiny step.

In my own case, if after resolving each day I would get dressed, I had then tried to get back into television, I would have landed flat on my face. I had neither the self-confidence nor the energy to try to fight the television battles. Though I might be getting dressed, I remained convinced that I would never work in television again.

Instead I kept my goals low and my focus intense. My goal was to get dressed every day. Once I got good at that, then I would see how it went putting on makeup. If I became accomplished at putting myself together, I might try to go out of the house.

While I've been writing this, I've been sharing my work with Karl. (You don't think I'd say all these personal things without letting him check it out first, do you?)

He read the part about the day I was so demoralized that I couldn't even feed the baby. It's funny, but while that day stands in my mind as a major turning point, it barely registered to him.

"Oh, yeah," he said with some hesitation. "I remember that day."

"Did you know it was when I turned the corner and started getting better?" I asked.

"No," he replied.

"Well, when did you think things were starting to change for me?" I was curious to hear his take on how I'd started putting all the tough times behind me.

"It was the first time when you left the house," Karl declared with absolute certainty. "I remember you were going to meet someone someplace. I knew then that you were getting better."

It was a small baby step. But it was the first step on a journey toward recovery that's left me feeling not only like my old self, but stronger. Able to take on the challenges that would have seemed impossible before.

"I can't believe I did this without falling to pieces. If you had told me on April 18 that all of this would happen on April 19, I would have said, 'Well, you'll have to visit me at the nuthouse because I can't handle it.'"

For all Americans, April 19, 1995, is a date engraved in our collective memories. April 19, 1995—the day terrorism struck at the heart of America. The day the Alfred P. Murrah Federal Building was destroyed by a bomb in Oklahoma City. Caye Allen's husband, Ted, was one of the 168 people who were killed.

The day started for Caye and Ted just like any other day. The usual chaos of trying to get kids out of bed, dressed, and out the door to school—and then still get to work on time themselves. Ted, aged forty-eight, worked for the Department of Housing and Urban Development. Caye worked just four blocks away at the U.S. Attorney's office.

Married six years, the Allens were a "yours, mine, and ours" kind of family with a total of six children between them: Ted's children from his first marriage, Jill, then twenty-two, Gretchen age twenty, Spencer age seventeen, and sixteen-year-old Megan, Caye's thirteen-year-old daughter, Rachel, from her previous marriage, with Caye and Ted's four-year-old, Austin, bringing up the rear. As Caye puts it, "Something's always going on around here!"

It was the kind of April morning that jolts you into realizing winter is more than just a memory. Spring is behind you and summer is just a heat wave away. The Allens' thoughts were beginning to focus on some of the end-of-the-school-year rituals that were approaching. Cheerleading tryouts and Spencer's upcoming prom had been regular topics of conversation.

For Caye, this particular Wednesday represented a bit of a break in routine and a chance to spend a few extra minutes with Ted. Her car was due in the shop that day for maintenance. So Caye and Ted would drive to work together in his white pickup truck after leaving her car with the mechanic. That break in routine has found Caye asking, "What if . . ." more than once.

"We got there at five till nine," Caye remembers. "Normally, we'd have been there at 8:30. If we'd done that, normally at nine o'clock he'd have been across the street at the coffee shop. He always went over there every day at nine. But, because we were running late, I guess he didn't feel he had the time for that.

"We were in his truck—his shrine—and as I dropped him off, he said, 'Don't hit any curbs with my tires!' And I said, 'Gee, Ted, you love this truck more than you love me!' And he got a kick out of that and started to laugh and said, 'God Caye!' and walked on in the building."

That was the last Caye saw of her husband.

Five minutes later, Caye was in her office four blocks away, just putting a bagel into the microwave, when the entire building shook.

"You could see the windows move in and out. Everyone came running and said, 'What was that?'" Caye goes on: "We thought the Chic-Fil-A across the street had a gas leak, but then this guy comes walking down the hall and he said, 'I've been to Vietnam, that was a bomb.' And I said, 'Oh, don't be silly, it was not.' And Nick looked at me and said, 'Yes, it *was,* Caye. *That* was a bomb.'"

With the rest of her co-workers, Caye ran to a window on the other side of the building where thick black smoke could be seen pouring from something to the north. Thousands upon thousands of tiny pieces of paper rained through the smoke. Caye still doesn't know why she ran toward the smoke, but she grabbed a girlfriend and headed toward the street. What she found was as surreal as any movie set.

Cars were crumpled as though they were made of aluminum foil, their windows shattered from the sonic blast. Shards of glass covered the street. As Caye and her friend walked toward where they thought the blast had come from, they were met by first a trickle and then a stream of people walking toward them. Wounded. Dazed. In shock.

"The strangest thing about it all was the silence." Caye is cradling her youngest son, Austin, as she speaks. "It was completely silent. There was no noise. Nobody was talking. Not a one of those kids was crying. There was nothing."

Moments later, the silence ended, interrupted by the sound of sirens. Their shrill scream began ripping through the air in an unending sound. Wave after wave, the sirens wailed their incessant calls for help.

As Caye worked her way toward the blast site, she was still trying to figure out just what had happened. And where. The closer she and her friend got, the more intense the heat. "What could have made such an explosion and created such incredible heat?" she wondered. The only answer that came to mind was perhaps a tanker car had exploded in the parking lot near the courthouse.

Like the rest of America, Caye Allen had never considered the possibility that a bomb would go off in her midst.

After about ten horrifying minutes watching children being pulled from the day care center and seeing officeworkers who only minutes before had been calmly going about their jobs now emerge bloodied and cut, Caye understood what had happened. The realization became more clear that something had exploded in the Murrah Federal Building. The building where less than twenty minutes earlier, she and Ted had joked about who he loved most: his wife or his truck.

"You couldn't get around to the front of that building because it was just too hot to get anywhere near it. I had no idea what the front of the building looked like until I saw the television news that night. I had no idea how bad it was . . ." Caye stops for a moment to take a stronger grip on the reins of control she is obviously struggling to hold.

"I knew by about noon that Ted was either dead or hurt very badly or he would have found me. He wouldn't have done that to me. I knew come hell or high water that within three hours he would have found a way to find me and tell me that he was okay.

"So I knew by noon that something bad, really bad, had happened. And I prayed that he was hurt. And, and . . ." Caye is losing the fight to keep back the tears. "And I believed that . . . until I saw the building on TV that night. The minute I saw the building I thought, 'That's it! He's gone.'

"When I saw what part of the building was destroyed, I knew that was Ted's office. But I didn't tell anybody. I didn't tell the kids. None of them knew. There was still this little bit of Pollyanna hope in me that he was in a some pocket of air. That they were going to find him—but I really didn't think so."

The next day, Caye tried to prepare the older children for the news she intuitively knew was to come. She told them the collapsed part of the building included the HUD offices where Ted worked. And Caye says she told them, "'You guys realize if there was any way your dad could get to us or get to a phone or get to anywhere, we would have heard something.' And they knew that was the way Ted was."

But preparing little Austin for the grim possibility was another matter. He was just four and a half. He worshipped his daddy. And it was making Caye physically sick to think about how Austin would react to the news.

She stopped eating. For four days, every time Caye tried to eat something, she gagged reflexively. From Wednesday when the bomb exploded until Sunday, Caye went without sleep. It was only Sunday night, when she finally explained to Austin that Daddy was probably in the building that exploded and probably wouldn't be coming home, that she found peace. Caye slept for the first time in days.

"How did you handle it?" I asked her.

"Well, you just do." Caye has this amazing matter-of-factness in the way she speaks. And in the way she approaches life. "When you have kids you have no other choice. What else can you do? Lie down and curl into a ball? Because if *you* don't handle it, who's going to do it?

"I would tell myself, 'Stay in control. You will get through this, but you have to stay in control for yourself and your family.' And by that, I don't mean emotionless.

"I feel you have to set the tone—not the example—but you have to set the tone. And the tone I chose to set was: 'We have been blessed.' We lost a lot, but we had so much more than most people had. We had so much before we lost him. And I would rather have had that, than to have nothing at all."

Ted's daughter Jill was the first to grasp what Caye was trying to do.

"She made a comment to a reporter," Caye recalls. "And she said she was so lucky because she had her dad for twenty-two years and Austin only had him for four."

The only thing worse than a quitter is the person who is afraid to begin.

When I first met Caye in that church parking lot in Oklahoma City, I remembered looking at the photo she had of her and Ted and their family and thinking, "This just isn't fair." The Allens made such an attractive family and it was obvious from the way Caye brightened when she spoke of her husband just how much she loved and looked up to him. His death just wasn't fair.

It was the same thought I had the first time I met Jana: "This isn't fair."

Jana's a pretty, perky blonde who looks so much like me we could be sisters. She's got blue eyes that can pierce right through you and a drive and determination that mean success in any area can be hers.

And when she's on the basketball court, you don't want to be between her and the hoop: she'll mow you down!

Oh. Did I mention that Jana's confined to a wheelchair? *That's* the part that's not fair.

At the age of fifteen, when most teenage girls are concerned about whether they'll be invited to the prom and why they are taller than all the boys, Jane was presented with a much bigger question: what is life in a wheelchair going to be like?

The day started out like any other. It was the last day of her freshman year in high school in Belleville, Kansas, a tiny rural town. For Jana it had been a great year, with the highlights on all her athletic pursuits. She'd made the cheerleading squad and the show choir. She'd performed as a majorette in the twirling corps. She made the basketball team.

After school dismissed for the summer, Jana accompanied a girlfriend to a party in a nearby farming community. The two girls were approaching a railroad crossing when the car spun out of control. The rear end hit the embankment and Jana was thrown from the front passenger seat to the back when her seatback collapsed.

While Jana lay unconscious, her friend ran to find help. Jana awoke with excruciating back pain, unable to move her legs.

"I thought, 'I can't walk.' I remember thinking, 'Am I paralyzed?' And it was weird to me because I didn't really know anybody who was paralyzed. I thought about the past, my twirling lessons and my basketball and gymnastics and dance lessons and all that stuff. Finally I just stopped and said the Lord's Prayer."

When the ambulance finally arrived, Jana was rushed to the local hospital where doctors discovered she had broken her back at the fourth vertebra on the thoracic or chest part of the spine. The next hours were a blur as Jana was rushed to a more state-of-the art-hospital in Salina, Kansas, and doctors began what proved to be a futile fight to help her regain some mobility in her legs.

Jana was sure she felt her toes and legs moving. The doctors told her it was psychosomatic—much the same as an amputee who can still feel a missing limb. When even the most sophisticated tests showed no trace of movement, the doctors shared the grim news.

"I can still remember the day when they told me I would probably never feel or move again." Jana sighs as she shares her story. "That was probably the hardest day in the hospital. I stayed up all night and I just cried. It seemed like all my life up to that point I had focused on and worked on things that I would no longer be able to do. That was *so* hard!"

And it got worse. Two metal rods were inserted into her back to stabilize her spine. The rest of her body was confined by a brace. Every twenty minutes she was turned to prevent bedsores. When they finally allowed her to try sitting up, the change in equilibrium made her violently nauseous.

Most of all, the pain was unbearable. The painkillers were not nearly effective enough. "I was hooked up to a machine where I could give myself pain reliever every eight minutes. They had it timed so I couldn't overdose. I can remember just watching the clock for my eight minutes to be up so I could push it again. It was really horrible."

Jana kept a journal during those initial dark days in the hospital. She was kind enough to share it with me, and with her permission, I'll repeat some of it here.

It begins:

This is only temporary.
On May 23, 1990, I feel as if the world caved in on my life. The only thing in my mind from then on was being able to walk again. After I achieve that goal I will go on from there. . . . Just between us, I honestly wish I were dead. Things would be so much easier. Nobody will ever truly know the pain I have already suffered.

But the entry ends:

The minute I start to give up so will my friends and family. I won't let anybody down. I am Jana Stump.

Why? It was a question that repeated itself over and over and over again in Jana's mind as she lay in her hospital bed. The answer never came.

"It was worse at night," she recalls. "When my mom was there during the day, we'd talk and she'd keep my mind occupied. And there were so many tests and X-rays and doctors and nurses always doing things to me. At night, it was different."

At night Jana was alone. Alone with her thoughts and her unanswered questions. She lay there, confined by her body and her braces, listening to the constant hum of the machines that were monitoring her vital signs. The darkness of the room was broken by the eerie green glow from the display panels of the machines.

Jana's diary reflects the emotions that were at war within her. On the day she first sat in a wheelchair, she writes, "It hurts so bad to know that people now consider me handicapped."

The day the doctors gave her little hope of ever walking, she says, "I wish our emotions could be like light switches where we could turn them on and off."

And ten days later: "I want to begin the plot of my suicide."

It was not until Jana arrived at Craig Hospital in Colorado Springs, Colorado, that she started to turn the corner. "I saw so many people who had such worse disabilities," she says. "I saw people whose injuries were so high they couldn't even smile. I remember this guy the first day I got there. He asked me if I could itch his nose for him. I guess it hit me: this isn't so bad."

Jana's change in attitude was the first small, tentative step she took toward getting her life back on track. But it has been a trip that in many ways has been two steps forward and one step back. At the rehabilitation hospital, Jana seemed one of the more able-bodied patients. When the people around her seemed so profoundly disabled in comparison to her injury, she was able to imagine an independent life: driving a car, going to college, something approaching normal.

But back at school, to Jana the emphasis was on her deficits. She was different. A freak. An oddity.

Jana was still on the cheerleading squad and in the show choir. But *everything* was different.

"I was a good actress. I would get on the football field and do these cheers with the rest of the squad and do these dances and it looked like I was having a blast and I *was* having fun—but there was always a little part of me—I knew people were staring at me." Jana pauses for a long time before she finishes her thought. "I feel like I've had to grow up a lot faster than I would have."

And as part of that growing up, Jana realized that she didn't have to give up all her goals. She simply had to give up her old game plan on how she would reach them.

"Before my accident, I was Jana the basketball player, Jana the baton twirler. After my accident, I was Jana, the one in the wheelchair."

Then Jana got a new label. A label she won and wore proudly. Two years after her accident, she was named Kansas's Junior Miss. She represented her state at the America's Junior Miss pageant. With a laugh, Jana looks back on the experience as "probably the best moment of my life." It was the turning point in which Jana finally felt she was back on track.

"I felt like people in the audience were thinking, 'Look at that girl, she's in a wheelchair.' But then the girls voted me the Spirit Award winner. I got a standing ovation from the crowd and all the judges. It was such a self-esteem booster. The community made me feel like I *deserved* that award!"

Entering the competition was a real challenge for Jana. There were stares and whispers. She heard the furtive "How's she going to do *that?*" as a stage routine was demonstrated. Jana says she tried to keep her eye focused on her goal. Winning the contest, she now says, was more than just reaching a goal—it was tangible proof that a wheelchair didn't mean *everything* in life would be different.

And that gave Jana confidence to set for herself even higher goals. "If a wheelchair didn't mean I'd have to give up my dream of competing for Junior Miss, I figured maybe I didn't have to give up athletics," Jana explained. "So I decided I was going to make the Olympic basketball team."

I guess no one reading will be surprised to hear that last August Jana Stump was one of the members of Team USA competing in the Paralympic Games in Atlanta.

Jana's journey has taken her places that days after her accident she could have never imagined she would go. From those weeks of traction in a hospital bed in Kansas, she has bounced back to represent her country in international athletic competition.

"I feel like I've gone on with my life and I've even made more with my life than I would have if I hadn't gone through this situation. I feel like I've achieved more than I would in able-bodied basketball."

"Desire accomplished is sweet to the soul."

—Proverbs 13:19

Jana never lay in her hospital bed imagining one day she'd be competing for a spot on an Olympic team. Striving to sit up was enough of a goal.

When her husband walked out, Robin might have dreamed about beginning a new romantic life with another man—but first she had to stop crying.

I never thought about working in television again. I just wanted to be able to leave the house.

Start small, think tiny. The world will spin on its axis without any assistance from you.

Let your goals be tiny and seemingly insignificant. Yet when you achieve that first little goal, revel in it as though you've just won the Academy Award. "Desire accomplished is sweet to the soul." A goal achieved is a treat when you're hurting. Savor it and enjoy it.

The first time Jana Stump saw a wheelchair brought into her hospital room, she was filled with revulsion. "I am *not* handicapped!" she screamed. But transferring herself from her bed into that chair was a first and not insignificant step toward the full life she now enjoys.

The two months after the Oklahoma City blast are something of a haze for Caye Allen.

"I did not read a paper, I could not watch the news," she says. The airwaves and newspapers were filled with information about the victims and the latest on the investigation. "I just put all the papers from April 19 until about the middle of July in a big box. I keep telling myself I'm going to take a week and just go through everything and see what I missed, but . . ." She sighs. "I just can't bring myself to do it. I keep coming up with something else to do instead."

It was much the same when it came to going back to work. The last time Caye had been in her office at the U.S. Attorney's office was the morning of the blast. For all she knew, her bagel was still in the microwave where she left it. Going back to work, being in the office just four blocks from the place where her husband was killed was a prospect that was simply paralyzing.

Somehow Caye's pragmatism won out over the paralysis.

"I just knew if I was ever going to get back to some kind of normalcy in our lives, I was going to have to go back to work. I went back after eight weeks and I still wasn't ready. But I just felt like if I didn't go back, I would never take that step to being normal.

"It was June 12 . . ." As Caye talks, her voice drifts away. You can tell she's reliving that painful step back toward her old life.

"It was hard," she says, taking a deep breath. "It was hard on everybody. Nobody knew what to say. People would come up to me and you knew they'd thought about what they wanted to say, but then they would see me and they'd start crying. The minute they'd turn the corner to my office, they'd just lose it.

"I went back that first day and on the way I thought, 'I just cannot do this,'" she recalls. And yet when Caye arrived at her office, she found that her co-workers had gone all out to make the office seem warm and welcome—and safe. They'd filled her office with more than a hundred balloons and hung welcome signs everywhere.

"By two or two-thirty I was okay. And I thought the next day,

I *can* do this." Caye took inspiration from the small fact that she was actually back in her office. Just being there—and staying—was fuel to help her accomplish the next challenge.

"When it started out, it was, 'I'm going to go to work.' And the next thing was, 'I will be in on time.' And then—'I'll be on time two days in a row.' You can't jump in and be normal because you are *not* normal." Caye is emphatic on this point.

"One time, one of my goals was to drive to work without crying. And the next day, I will try to drive to and from work without crying."

It has been a long road back for Caye and she knows she's still not there yet. "Some days I'll just tell myself that I'm not going to look out the window. If I'd just glance out, it would be ten minutes that I'd be sitting there staring. I guess I've learned to just take things one day at a time."

And one day at a time, Caye Allen is getting her life and those of her children back on track. There is no disputing the loss they've suffered. There is no way the emptiness Ted's death left can be filled. But the Allen family *is* living. Not just existing.

Caye will go to great pains to tell you she's okay. But she doesn't pretend everything is all right. "I feel like a big portion of me is missing. I feel comfortable with myself in that I feel complete, although I wish my other half were still here."

Caye's Oklahoma roots helped her come up with a good analogy. "It's like being a three-legged dog. You adapt. A dog with three legs walks like he's always been like that. I have now learned to walk on three legs and it feels natural. I have adapted to my situation."

Chapter Four

IT'S OKAY TO INHALE

"The messier my life is, the cleaner my closets become."

MY CUPBOARDS WERE THE CLEANEST they'd ever been when I was in the midst of the *Today* show nonsense. As I was struggling to get control of my life again, I would often recognize the signs that I was once more slipping into the panic mode.

No breath was ever quite deep enough. My heart would start to race. I'd think about one thing only to jump over to another thought before I had time to complete the first one. My conversation was the same way: a staccato, rapid-fire volley of often disconnected thoughts.

It was as though I'd think or talk about one topic just long enough to bounce to the next one. In reality I never really completed a thought about anything.

"Relax!" Karl would implore. "Just disconnect your mind," he would urge as I tossed and turned in bed, fully expecting another night of elusive sleep.

That was easy for him to say! A person in crisis cannot disconnect her mind. It's the one thing she *can* control, she can rely on. Switching off your mind might prevent you from coming up with the very solution that will end the crisis. Instead the wheels turn faster and faster and those mental computer chips seem to go into overdrive.

"Things are happening and I can't control them!" you think in near panic. "I've got to do something!"

Hold it! What you've got to do is get off the running wheel. Channel that frenetic, unfocused energy. Slow down.

I remember one particular day at NBC. It was the day a lot of people on the early shift had been waiting for: the day I overslept. About seven or eight months into my job as anchor of *Sunrise,* all the fail-safe systems I had in place to make sure that I got up in the morning—failed! The alarm didn't go off (or more likely, I turned it off in my sleep), I slept through the phone call from the office, the doorman didn't buzz me.

When I woke up, the clock read 5:30 A.M. In twenty-nine minutes, I was supposed to be on nationwide television telling the country what was going on the world! So what did I do? I stood in the bedroom naked as a jay bird and just ran in place in panic.

"I've got to get to work! I can't get to work!" I panted as I ran. "They're going to kill me at work. I've got to get to work!"

I was filled with the adrenaline of panic—and just stood there spinning my wheels. Karl settled things. "Either go to work or get in bed, but be quiet," he growled.

I went to work.

And I made it. Did my makeup in the car, dashed into the makeup room where Jane Pauley and John Palmer were laughing at me.

"We wondered when it would happen to you," Jane chuckled. "Everyone always sleeps through the show at some point. "I remember once when Tom Brokaw didn't make it to *Today* until about twenty minutes to eight!"

A crisis will leave most of us similarly running in place—but it's not nearly so amusing. When crisis hits, you want to do something—anything—to make it go away.

"Surely there is something I can do!" you frantically declare to yourself. And that begins a mad, usually fruitless dance to find the solution to the problem.

"I was for him in whatever his endeavors were. My goal was just to be Mrs. David Green."

When Cynthia married David Green seventeen years ago, she was reaching her life's goal. She had earned a degree in sociology and social work, but her ambition was simply to be her husband's helpmate. He was studying for a career in the ministry and while David worked on his graduate degree, Cynthia earned extra credits at school or took various jobs to help ends meet.

Money was not a focus of theirs. Cynthia looked forward to David's earning his degree and being assigned a church. She'd have the opportunity to serve as a minister's wife, helping her husband and members of the congregation.

In the beginning it all seemed to be working out beautifully. They saw God's hand at work when they were assigned to a church in Nashville, just a few hours' drive from their hometown.

"We were just praying for east of the Mississippi," Cynthia remembers. "We never dreamed we would be just two hours from home!"

For a while, everything for Cynthia and David seemed absolutely perfect. David's dream of becoming a youth minister had been realized. With some help from their families, they sold their first house and bought a beautiful Cape Cod style home with everything Cynthia ever wanted: a spacious master bedroom and bath, a library, eat-in kitchen, and formal dining room.

But then, four and a half years into his work as a minister, David realized something was wrong. He wasn't as fulfilled in his post as he thought he should be. He'd lost his direction in life. He wasn't happy. The other ministers and leaders of the church saw his unhappiness and asked to meet with him.

"I remember that night so clearly," Cynthia says. "It was August. I was sweeping the master bathroom and David walked in and I looked at him and I said, 'Something has happened tonight.' And somehow I knew. I said, 'You quit your job!' And he said, 'Sit down, we have got to talk.'"

David confirmed that, indeed, the church elders had asked him to relinquish his position. They knew the young minister was not happy in his position, but thought so highly of David and Cynthia that they offered to continue paying his salary until the end of the year.

"So," Cynthia explains, "now we had to figure out what we were going to do. Then David said he'd always wanted to sell high-end cars—luxury cars like Mercedes and Porches and BMWs.

"It really floored me. I mean, to go from the ministry to selling cars . . . ! This is like going from opposite ends of the spectrum! I thought, 'There is nothing stable about this.' And that is what is so uncharacteristic of David because he is so solid. I'm talking 'rock of Gibraltar.'"

David may be solid, but the car business was certainly not. On a minister's salary, the Greens hardly had the resources to open an automobile business. But David's family was financially comfortable and David was able to persuade his parents to let him borrow against his future inheritance to open a dealership selling gently used luxury cars.

David teamed up with a church friend who had experience in the auto business. The friend put in his expertise, while David, whose parents were *more* than generous, pledged close to one million dollars of his parents' stock portfolio as collateral for bank loans to open the business.

By December, they'd leased a location, purchased tools and office equipment and cars, and were open for business.

Cynthia talks with pride about the vehicles they sold. "They were *better* than new by the time we were finished with them. We wouldn't buy trash. They had to be in top running order or we wouldn't touch them."

With a few predictable fits and starts, the business was going well. Then ten months after opening, the bottom fell out of the stock market. When Cynthia heard about the October 19, 1987, stock market collapse, she anticipated tough times ahead: after all, who buys luxury cars during a market decline? But she never expected what actually happened.

"I just didn't realize we were that far into debt. The bank called the loan immediately," Cynthia remembers. In the space of a few hours, the value of the stock pledged against the bank loans was cut in half. The bank would not consider extending the loan and David's parents were suddenly in no position to help out any further. There was nothing to do but try to liquidate the car dealership immediately.

"We spent the next two and a half months selling everything," Cynthia says. "We were driving all the way to Montgomery, Alabama, to sell cars off the lot—anywhere we could go to get rid of inventory. We had to find somebody to buy the car lifts. We had two of those at $15,000 a pop. We had to get rid of those.

"Then there were all those tools. We had tools that had never even been used, so we had to find out if the tool company would buy them back from us. It was constantly talking with somebody about buying something or trading for something or 'You take these and try to sell it for us.'"

It didn't take long for the stress of it all to take its toll. With no source of income, the Greens were facing a $4,000 to $5,000 monthly payment for the lease on a car dealership they no longer operated. Then they needed another $500 for their house payment, . . . $99 per month for the fax machine rental they were stuck with. And so on. The bills kept piling up. Their partner bailed out on them. The Greens' marriage was suffering as much as their finances.

"Our marriage was crumbling," Cynthia remembers. "It wears on you to go to the grocery store and not know if you'll be able to afford everything you want to put in that basket. To not get a haircut because you're afraid to spend the money."

As each piece of the business was sold, David grew more despondent. So much so that Cynthia hid her own feelings and feigned strength when, in fact, she too had lost her anchor.

"I would hold David at night when he cried himself to sleep in the bed. I was also falling apart, but I couldn't let him know. I was having a nervous breakdown."

"How did you know?" I asked Cynthia.

"I sensed it . . ." Cynthia paused, uncertain whether to continue. "I sensed it, because I started drinking."

Throughout her life, Cynthia says she has seen liquor destroy the man she'd grown up loving and respecting—her father. She'd watched alcohol wash away opportunity after opportunity for him. Mindful of the tendency for alcoholism to run in families, Cynthia had always stayed clear of liquor. Until now.

Unable to share her fears with her husband, embarrassed to confide in her friends, Cynthia's solace came in a six-pack. She knew she was losing her grip.

STEP THREE TO GETTING BACK ON TRACK: GET CONTROL

Whatever the source of your crisis, there is no way you can deal with it effectively if you're running away from the problem or around like a maniac. You cannot change your situation if you cannot focus on it. And the breathless rush to do something/anything will only increase the anxiety that you feel now.

You've got to get control by slowing down that racing motor of yours.

Relax. Chill. Take a powder.

Call it what you will—but give it your complete focus. Tell yourself, I *will* get off the merry-go-round. And then *do it!*

For the longest time, it seemed Cynthia and David just couldn't buy a break. They put their dream house up for sale, but doing so just after the market crash was the worst possible timing.

"What was your biggest fear?" I asked Cynthia.

"I think my biggest fear was that David was going to die of a heart attack. To this day, nothing scares me more than David dying and leaving me. Sometimes at night I'll just wake up and reach out to make sure he's there and he's breathing!" Cynthia laughs.

"My next greatest fear was that he had grown up in a certain lifestyle. He was not accustomed to having to watch every penny and I wondered how he was going to survive it. I didn't think he could handle a life of less than financial plenty."

"You knew you could?" I said.

"Yeah," Cynthia replied. "I grew up in a middle-class family. I had everything I wanted, but I watched my parents work some of the strangest hours and work their fingers to the bone to take care of me and my brother. I figured I could survive it."

As David became more withdrawn, Cynthia spent more time with alcoholic beverages. Then one morning she woke up with a splitting headache and said to herself, "This is stupid!" She knew the current situation was hurting both of them. So she left.

She went to visit some old college friends in Texas. As she got on the plane, Cynthia wasn't sure she'd be coming back. She spent much of her ten-day visit in Texas talking. She talked endlessly about the debacles with the business, her fears about her husband, her concern for her marriage. For long hours, they talked about what had happened and gradually the magnitude of it all seemed to diminish. Cynthia began to sense maybe she *could* handle this after all.

"I said to myself, 'You've been queen of your pity pot now for a while. It's time to decide if you're going home or not and when you make this decision to go home, you are going *home.*'" And so she did. Cynthia and David's problems were far from resolved, but she had gotten control of the uncertainty of their relationship. She flew home determined to make her marriage—and their financial lives—whole again.

"I kept thinking about something my brother said once when he went through a really tough time," Cynthia explains. "He said, 'I will crawl until I can walk and I will walk until I can run.' And that's the way I felt. I said, 'I'm going to stand and then walk and when I'm really well, I'm going to run again.' We just took it one step at a time."

• • •

"All the external signs were 'it's over.' It's done. Get on with life. The world was just the way I had left it. The only thing that was different was me. And that just added to the unreality of it."

Marcia Johnson's day was one that began and ended much like any other workday. She woke up, went to work, and since she didn't have a date, Marcia busied herself with chores around her small but tidy garden apartment. There was laundry to be done, the plants on the patio needed watering. Marcia tended to all these things and was, in fact, so taken by this burst of domesticity that, before falling asleep, she even repaired some loose buttons on a shirt.

It was a day that was remarkably unmemorable in the life of a twenty-five-year-old single woman just embarking on her career. That is, it *was,* until several hours after Marcia fell asleep.

"He woke me up. I awakened to feel a hand over my mouth and he said, 'Don't scream and I won't kill you. Don't scream and I won't hurt you.' And he removed his hand. I just remember trying to shake myself awake. If I wake up, he won't be here."

Time hasn't dulled Marcia's recollections of that night. She recounts the details of her assault with a precision that would have certainly landed her assailant in jail—if only the police had caught him.

The bedroom was illuminated by the eerie blue light of the television. Marcia had fallen asleep with the set on. In the wee hours of the morning when the intruder woke her up, the snowy picture on the screen put out enough light for Marcia to see him clearly.

"He was white, young—I would say late twenties, early thirties. He had very thick curly hair. His features were just very *average*. You could see that this was a person who could just fail all his life. There was a bit of the ninety-pound weakling there."

There was never any chance of escape. When Marcia woke up, the man was already astride her on the bed. There seemed little possibility of talking her way free of him: the light of the television caught a glint of metal in his hand. Was it a knife? A gun? Marcia never knew.

For a moment, the thought flashed through her head: the scissors! The scissors she'd used earlier to sew on a button were still on the nightstand. But then the thought—don't antagonize him. As a numbing, disbelieving paralysis set in, Marcia was consumed by one thought—and one alone: *I want to live. I just want to live!*

It was a sickening episode. Not violent. Sickening.

"He made these remarks that sounded so perverse and so obscene. They just added to the unreality of the situation. He kept talking about wanting to give me pleasure. 'Does this please you? Do you like it when I do this? You're more beautiful than I'd imagined you would be. I've waited so long for your body.'"

It was soap opera dialogue. To hear these tender remarks from a lover would have brought tremendous pleasure to Marcia or any other woman. But uttered during such a cruel violation, it was revolting. It only added to the unreality Marcia was already experiencing.

It lasted twenty minutes. Marcia doesn't remember crying.

She knows she didn't scream. She was frozen with fear.

"I couldn't think beyond the next moment. All I could think is . . . 'What is he going to want next?' That I just wanted to live. And—I was afraid what would happen when he finished."

When it was over, the man got up. He took a large towel from the stack of freshly laundered items and covered Marcia from head to toe.

He said, "Do not get up. Do not call the police." And he was gone. No footsteps. No sounds of a door closing. He was just gone.

Marcia can't tell you how long she lay on the bed, covered like a corpse. Eventually she got up. She called her best friend, Bill—the fellow she'd been dating, though it was not yet a serious relationship.

"The minute he walked in, he said, 'I think I know what happened. I want you to tell me and then I want to call the police.' Which we did."

Bill was there—for everything. He held her hand during the rape exam at the hospital. He nursed her through the excruciating side effects of the morning-after drugs she was given. He got her out of her apartment and let her stay in his. He found a new and safe place for her to live.

He phoned Marcia's absence to her boss and he broke the news to her parents. The first time Bill spoke with Marcia's mother and father, it was to tell them their daughter had been raped.

Physically, Marcia healed. Emotionally, she was completely rudderless. It was the crisis she never expected to happen.

"I lost my sense that nothing is inviolate. I was a twenty-something who thought nothing bad will happen. Nothing bad ever *did* happen to me. Gosh, you know, when I didn't make cheerleader I made captain of the drill team. Somehow I always came out okay. Part of me said, just get up and get on with it. Come out okay."

But the other part of Marcia, the part that won the battle for her emotions, was terrified. He—whoever *he* was—was still out there. Throughout the rape, he'd described how he'd been watching Marcia. For all she knew, he was still there. Still watching. Perhaps, waiting for his chance to return.

There was no way Marcia could let down her guard. No chance she could possibly relax.

"Live in each season as it passes, breathe the air, drink the drink, taste the fruit . . . be blown on by all the winds."

—Henry David Thoreau

Wouldn't life be wonderful if we could really do what Thoreau admonishes? Ignore *real* life and just blissfully wander from day to day partaking of life's good things—undisturbed by the stresses that are a part of life in the 1990s. Of course, Thoreau lived in another century, in another time. Heck, he even abandoned city life of the 1860s and lived in the woods for a while.

Easy for him to say, "Drink the drink, taste the fruit." After all, who's going to earn the bucks to buy all that wine and fruit, right?

Real life, we all know, doesn't work that way. One can't walk away from the emotional scars, the sick children, the physical injuries, or the crashed careers and marriages and "taste the fruit." *Or can we?*

You may not be able to abandon your busy life and hightail it to Walden Pond, but you can uncomplicate your life—and destress it.

In his book *Freedom from Stress,* Dr. Phil Nuernberger says that the way we breathe plays a vital role in whether or not we are affected by stress. And in fact, every stress-reducing exercise I've encountered involves controlled breathing to some extent. The trick is *how* we breathe.

As a kid in elementary and junior high school, I played the flute in the school band. I liked the instrument—besides, it had the smallest case so it was the easiest to haul around! Our instructor, Mickey Fisher, stressed breathing above all else.

I can still hear the twitter of the students as Mr. Fisher demonstrated the difference between diaphragmatic breathing—which he wanted us to do—and thoracic breathing, which seemed to be all we could figure out. As Mr. Fisher breathed in, demonstrating the use of the diaphragm in breath control, his tummy grew more and more distended. It was incredible! You'd think the man was pregnant!

And yet, as he demonstrated, he could hold a note seemingly *hours* longer when using diaphragmatic breathing, filling his abdominal cavity with much more oxygen than he could using traditional chest or thoracic breathing. He always finished his thoracic breathing demonstration red in the face and out of breath. But Mr. Fisher seemed completely at ease with diaphragmatic breathing— plus he held a note much, *much* longer.

There is no difference in the amount of oxygen used by the body whichever way you breathe. But there is a huge difference in the workload the body expends. In fact, the lungs and cardiovascular system must work 50 percent harder when we use thoracic or chest breathing. Any guesses which kind of breathing exercise I'm going to recommend you try?

Remember, as you try some of the relaxation exercises, try to practice diaphragmatic breathing. That means allowing the oxygen to fill the lower lungs, letting your diaphragm expand downward toward the abdomen. Properly done, your tummy will actually begin to expand outward. (Yes, I know this is completely opposite to everything we women are attempting to do by constantly holding our tummies in to look slim. Forget slimness for the moment, we're trying to relax.)

If your shoulders are rising significantly or your upper chest expanding—you're not breathing correctly. Concentrate on filling the *lower* part of your lungs, letting your belly expand.

Relaxation Exercise No. 1: Ten-Count Breathing

My own particular on-the-spot relaxation technique is actually something I was taught by a guest on the newscast I anchored in Chicago. It's quite simple and works beautifully for those panicky attacks that leave you fidgeting and worried about what's next.

It takes less than a minute.

First of all, close your eyes and try to tune out the distractions and noise you might hear. Slowly inhale, counting to ten as you breathe in. Pace yourself. You want your breathing to be even. Don't suck in all the air by the time you hit four, as you'll be bursting before you get to ten.

Once you've breathed in and reached ten, *hold* your breath for another ten count.

Then, ever so slowly, release the air. Breathe out slowly and evenly, pacing yourself so that the last bit of air escapes your lungs just as you're thinking . . . nine . . . and ten.

Now sit with your eyes closed a moment. You should feel a bit calmer. (A confession: as I am writing this, I am doing the breathing exercise and getting a bit drowsy.)

Relaxation Exercise No. 2: Letting Go Inch by Inch

My husband's method for relaxation works infuriatingly well for him. He closes his eyes and—BOOM! He's sound asleep. On those rare occasions in which he cannot fall asleep the moment he hits the pillow, he wills his body into relaxation.

He lies flat on his back and, beginning with his toes, he consciously relaxes every inch of his body. After "commanding" his toes and feet to relax, he gradually moves mentally up his body. Muscle by muscle, he isolates them in his mind and watches on his mind's television as each muscle releases the day's tension. He moves along his torso and out through his shoulders, biceps, and forearms. Finally his fingers become limp and he's well on his way to dreamland.

This is also the technique Jana Stump turns to when the stresses and hassles of trying to maneuver a wheelchair through a world of high curbs and stairs get the better of her.

Relaxation Exercise No. 3: A Mental Escape

This exercise allows you to mentally travel to a place where everything is pleasant and there is no stress. Imagine the most beautiful place you have ever been to. Picture the most incredible landscape you have ever seen in a photograph.

Close your eyes and mentally allow yourself to travel to your mental Shangri-la. Float through the air and land on the beach, plop in the hammock, swim in the stream. Picture yourself enjoying the scenery, breathing the fresh air, reveling in the coolness of the water—whatever is appropriate to your vision.

I have recommended this one to a friend who often lets the little stresses of the day build into a total frustration. Yet, when he pictures himself in his special place, he finds he is able to shrug off the things that are getting him uptight.

When Cynthia escaped the financial and emotional collapse of her marriage, her Texas friends encouraged her to meditate. They showed her a very simple exercise in which one spreads one's hands out—fingers wide—and then gently touch the fingertips together. Cynthia says as you slowly rub your fingertips in a circular motion, you should concentrate on your fingertips. This will gradually slow the breathing and clear the mind.

"It really does calm you and is one of the simplest things I've ever seen done," she raves.

By now, you've probably figured out I am not into this New Age "embrace your inner child" routine. So to read now that I'm encouraging you to try a few relaxation techniques might seem a bit out of character with the rest of my message. Not at all!

I want you to be *strong.* Able to take the reins of your life and steer yourself away from your current troubles. But before you do that, you've got to be able to clear the cobwebs from your brain, stop your heart from racing a mile a minute, and think effectively about which course of action will get you headed where you want to go.

Research conducted at Harvard University found that people who spend just a few minutes each day on stress-fighting techniques were healthier, more relaxed, and more alert than those who were buffeted by stress. You've had a crisis. You may still be in a crisis. To get beyond it and put it behind you, you must be strong. A few minutes spent now can help you become the winner you want to be in the future.

Remember it is *you* who will be charting this course—no one else. You want to make the best choices you can.

While step three to getting back on track is getting control, one of the ways you are going to do that is by *getting a grip, giving up,* and *letting go.* I know these sound at odds with each other, but stick with me here. This *will* make sense!

92

"I don't know the key to success, but the key to failure is trying to please everyone."

—Bill Cosby

You cannot be all things to all people. Don't even try.

This chapter is about relaxing. About slowing down, eliminating the stresses that we know are having a negative impact on our lives. Now is the time for you to heed the advice First Lady Nancy Reagan gave to teenagers confronted by drugs: "Just say no!"

Get control of your life by letting go of the feelings, responsibilities, the activities, and yes—the people who aren't part of the positive environment that will help you get back on track.

"I wish more than anything that I could give them my healthy body. If I could, I would—and they know that."

Susie Albert is the kind of woman a stranger would say has it all. She has cover girl looks, the perfect family—two boys and two girls—and a handsome and successful husband. She also has enormous guilt.

The girls are healthy. But both of Susie's sons have muscular dystrophy. It is the Duchenne strain of the disease, genetically linked through the X chromosome. Unless medical research makes tremendous strides, it is unlikely Susie's boys will live much into their thirties. And—as if the medical diagnosis weren't devastating enough—genetic testing has revealed the faulty gene that caused the disease came from their mother.

The boys' earliest years seemed perfectly normal. Jack was five and little Sammy just three when Susie and her husband, John, thought their younger son looked a bit odd when he was running through the backyard. They tried orthotics for his shoes. Another doctor suggested the toddler had pulled a muscle. Finally a third doctor suggested it might be a mild case of muscular dystrophy. An examination by a neurologist confirmed the hunch. And when doctors tested five-year-old Jack, who at that point had shown no signs of the disease, the diagnosis was the same. That was eight years ago.

"I guess you never really accept it," Susie says softly. "I think when I first found out, I didn't get my hopes up about a cure. It all seemed too devastating to me." Susie says her devastation was compounded when medical testing revealed that she had inherited from her father an incomplete gene that resulted in the boys' ill-nesses. Evidently her dad was exposed to an X-ray which damaged his sperm.

In those early days, when the Alberts weren't rushing from doctor to doctor trying to learn all they could about MD, Susie was trying to come to grips with an almost incapacitating sense of guilt.

"I feel badly for the boys that they are sick and that they got it from me. I wish that I didn't know they'd gotten it from me." There is a wistfulness in Susie's voice. "And for John, I'm . . . I don't know if it's feeling sorry or feeling guilty—but his life, because of me, is different from what it might have been having a healthy son. And he can't have a healthy son because of me.

"Dealing with the guilt? That's hard to say." Susie sips her coffee and pauses to think. "I *think* I've buried it in some ways—but not as well as I'd like to."

Though the guilt is mostly behind her, letting go of her anger has been more difficult. It was a bad roll of the genetic dice that left this suburban mother with a faulty gene to pass on to her sons. There was nothing, Susie realizes, she could have done to prevent it.

But it has been extremely difficult to be so sanguine about the question that Susie, like every other person in crisis still finds them-selves asking: "Why?"

"I mean *Why me?*" Susie's voice rises in anger as she thinks about it. "I look back on my life and I really haven't hurt many peo-ple. I really haven't made any major mistakes. I really *have* tried to be a good person! And I'm *really* telling the truth!"

Her voice lowers as Susie calms down, "I really didn't de-serve it."

Reflectively she adds, "In time, you start letting the anger go. You ask yourself, 'Where does it get you?'"

For Susie, letting go of the anger meant consciously reminding herself *not* to engage in those thoughts that produced nothing but higher blood pressure. For another woman, letting go might mean letting go of some of the myriad tasks that seem to become her responsibility on a daily basis.

Take a moment and chart out a typical day or, better yet, a typical week. It won't be that hard. Pull your calendar out of your purse and set it on the table. Then take your purse and dump it out, retrieving all those little scraps of paper on which you've written all the reminders to yourself about where you are supposed to be when.

Hour by hour, chart out the way you spend your time. Take a page or two in a spiral-bound notebook and put three columns across the top, with the hours running alongside the left margin of the page:

	Personal/Me	Personal/Home	Professional
6:00 a.m.			
7:00 a.m.			
8:00 a.m.			
9:00 a.m.			
10:00 a.m.			
11:00 a.m.			
12:00 noon			
1:00 p.m.			
2:00 p.m.			
3:00 p.m.			
4:00 p.m.			
5:00 p.m.			
6:00 p.m.			
7:00 p.m.			
8:00 p.m.			
9:00 p.m.			
10:00 p.m.			
11:00 p.m.			
12:00 midnight			

Go through your daily activities and mark them in the appropriate time column and heading.

After you've logged your day, go back and evaluate *how* your time is being spent. It may give you some clues to the lack of control you feel.

How much of your day is spent on things you *must* do? Work, running the household, paying bills, mothering your children, time with your husband. (If those last two aren't on your list as *must-do* items, they should be. It could be your crisis stems from putting your priorities in the wrong order.)

Now, look at the things you do because you *like* to do them. Are any of them contributing to your feeling of being over-whelmed? Perhaps you pride yourself on feeding your family fresh foods at all times. That is admirable, but if your desire to serve only garden-fresh food is putting *additional* pressure on yourself, may I suggest a visit to the frozen foods aisle? The selection is every bit as vast and with today's flash-freezing processes, very little is sacrificed in taste.

You'll find you have a real savings not only in price, but more important in wear and tear on yourself, leaving you more time for your family or leisure activities that *you* enjoy.

I've let go in a number of ways: in our backyard, there have been these two pathetic strips that purport to be a rose garden. Every year, Karl and I head over to the garden center and spend a small fortune on beautiful healthy rose bushes. Within two months' time, we're back at the garden center buying replacements for at least half of the bushes.

Everything about this bed of roses is wrong: the type of water it receives, its proximity to little boys' kickball games, and most crit-ically—the man and woman who pretend to be gardeners. The rose garden was so ugly that the day before Kyle was christened (and we were expecting guests to visit after the church service), Karl grabbed the wheelbarrow and pulled every one of the bushes out of the ground.

I've let go of the notion that we'll have a beautiful rose garden in those two strips. Karl still dreams on. But those two lines of bar-ren earth bugged me so much that one summer night, after I put the kids in bed, I sneaked outside with a bagful of grass seed and sowed a new lawn. It's a little patchy and I didn't get the seed planted too evenly in the darkness, but hey—that's one ugly rose garden that doesn't torment me anymore! (Unfortunately for Karl,

I've now created two hideous strips of lawn that are driving *him* nuts!)

I'll confess, saying no is easier said than done. While last summer I got a grip by letting go of those stupid roses, I still said yes (against my better instincts) to that request at church to sew up the angel costumes for the Christmas pageant. "Where," I asked myself as I was dragging home late from work, attending holiday parties with my husband, feeding the baby at four A.M. and then getting up at six o'clock, "was I going to find time to make fifteen angel outfits?"

I have to keep reminding myself of a pillow my grandmother once embroidered for me which said, "Please be patient, God isn't finished with me yet!" As you work to get back on track you will have lofty goals. Trust me—you will fail at times to reach them. After all, this job isn't finished yet.

What is it about your daily life that annoys the heck out of you? What *has* to be done and *you're* the one who has to do it that just drives you up a tree?

Am I the only one who hates meal planning? Surely my husband isn't the only man in America whose universal response to "What would you like for dinner?" is "Uh, I don't know."

I've got eight weeks' worth of menu plans in my computer. Now I never have to hassle about what to eat. And meal planning isn't a chore anymore. I zap out a week of menus (and the shopping list that goes with it) and my poor tired brain doesn't have to think.

I can't tell you how many women have offered to pay me for a copy of my menus. Meal planning *is* necessary, but it's an annoyance. Now it's an annoyance I've eliminated from my life.

Perhaps in your home, divvying up the week so different family members are in charge on different days would work. You might give up a bit in terms of nutrition, but the adventure of eating a meal selected by a twelve-year-old will be worth it! Just keep the vitamins handy.

GET CONTROL BY LETTING GO

You are no less a mother or wife if you bake brownies with a little help from the Pillsbury dough boy. If you've got children who are over the age of thirteen, let them take over some of the responsibilities of cooking and cleaning. Is mending a chore? Make it a family affair: imagine the laughs the entire family will have watching Dad try to sew on a button while your older daughter struggles to hem that skirt that *used* to always end up on *your* to-do pile. (You'll be doing her a favor. When she's out of the nest and learns what professionals charge to hem a skirt, she'll be thrilled you made her learn.)

Do you participate in school, community, or church activities out of a sense of obligation? Or do you truly feel fulfilled and accomplished by giving your time? If it gives you misgivings, then you should give it up. (Remember those angel costumes!)

Give up the idea that there is a right way to run your home. Forget the notion that paperwork in the office must be handled in a certain way. The message here is arrange your life/work/schedule so it works best for you—within the obvious constraints that exist. In many ways, this is more a change of mind-set than a change of activity.

Give yourself *permission* to do it differently. And then, give yourself Brownie points for doing the dreaded task. No matter how much you dislike numbers, the payroll report still has to be done by Thursday morning. You may be the ultimate night owl, but children still have to be taken to school in the morning. Change the way you look at the jobs you must do but can't stand.

It may be your mind-set that is what's really making the job difficult. Research has shown the more you procrastinate over a disagreeable task, the more your levels of adrenaline and other hormones fluctuate. This can actually work to create a state of high anxiety or mini-depression—which only reinforces one's lack of desire or resolve to attack a task.

Get Control by attacking the job. For many people the hardest part of getting out of bed in the morning is actually *getting* out of bed. After that, they coast through the morning. Once you push yourself into action, the hormone levels readjust, making the job you've been dreading actually easier to complete.

If you don't make good decisions in the morning, make most of your decisions the night before. Pick out your next day's outfit the night before. Match the shoes and the jewelry.

Don't forget to *reward* yourself for following through with the task. Last chapter we learned to take "little baby steps" to build our confidence and help us get through the day. Those baby steps haven't ended. You didn't want to pay those bills. You thought up every excuse in the book to avoid picking up the checkbook and a pen. But *you did it!* And now that you have, take a moment to reflect on that achievement. Pat yourself on the back—even if no one else does! You *know* you hate bill paying—and you did it anyway.

Be creative. I hate the phone, so I save up all my phone calls for one chunk of time when I can get them all done once during the day. I can't eliminate the need to talk on the phone—but now I try to do my talking on *my* terms when I'm geared up for it. When I have my phone-calling duties organized, it doesn't haunt me the way it used to.

Get control by letting go.

It may be that as you go through your daily calendar, you are struck with the notion that it is not *what* that is annoying and stressing you so much as *who!*

Some people are like Eeyore the donkey from *Winnie the Pooh*—always a little cloud of doom hovering over them. Like dirt is to Charlie Brown's pal Pig Pen, troubles just seem to cling to our human Eeyore. And the doom spreads. Put as much distance between you and Eeyore as you possibly can!

Is the great negative in your life that person who can never be pleased? It's like the mother-in-law who ignores the delicious dinner and comments that the linens you used weren't quite right. Or the husband whose wife gets a promotion, but his comment is that the raise isn't very much.

If you have an Eeyore in your life, ask yourself, "Is he/she saying this out of love and concern for me?" Are they trying to urge you on to be your best? Or are the remarks or gestures or body language really a subtle way of tearing you down to make themselves feel superior?

When Susan started a new job, one of her new female colleagues was tremendously warm and welcoming. She gave her advice about who to trust and who to watch out for. Greeted her every day with a warm smile and a little bit of news about the office.

"She was just a little too friendly," Susan says. "It just gave me the creeps. Since we were on the same level responsibility wise, I just didn't understand why she was going out of her way for me."

Later Susan began to notice her new office "friend" had wandering eye syndrome. Those friendly office chats always seemed to take place when Susan had all her paperwork spread on her desk. Susan knew her "pal" was trying to keep tabs on what she was doing in what seemed like an awfully competitive way.

"For the longest time, it really ate at me," Susan recalls. "I'd find myself thinking about her tricks when I wasn't at work and found that I was getting very suspicious, which just isn't like me."

Then Susan found a way to let go of her office mate's annoying curiosity. She laughs: "I started leaving fake memos on my desk that I knew would drive her nuts! She was so busy trying to track down the 'information' she snooped from my desk, she didn't have time to bother me when I was really working on something sensitive."

Susan couldn't get rid of her annoying co-worker, but she's found a way to let go of the annoyance.

In her previous job, Amanda was in a terrible situation. She knew her boss disliked her and was eager to replace her with his own person in her position. Every day, she would arrive at her office wondering what trap he'd set for her for the day. "He was just waiting for me to screw up so he could lower the boom," Amanda recalled. "I would walk into the office and as I entered the door, I could feel my body literally get tight. It's like I was bracing myself for what was to come."

With three children at home, Amanda could hardly quit her

101

job. But showing up for work was taking its toll. She began to experience a succession of headaches and back pain and a lack of energy.

"I knew I had to figure out some way to deal with this jerk," Amanda says. "So I would go into the ladies' room and lock myself in a stall. And then, while I was sitting there, I would close my eyes and imagine my boss in a boat."

Amanda breaks into a smile as she shares the rest of her visualization. "And I would just watch him drift further and further out to sea—without a motor, without an oar. He'd just drift further and further away to where he couldn't bother me."

LET GO OF NEGATIVE THINKING

Question: When the telephone rings, who do you figure is on the other end of the line? Someone waiting to tell you you've won the Publishers Clearinghouse prize—or your boss who wants to fire you? I've already 'fessed up to my phone phobia so you know which category I fall into!

"E-lim-i-nate the negative," as the old song goes—and that means negative thinking as well. You may never be able to stop expecting the worst when the telephone rings, but you *can* stop expecting every aspect of the day to be a tragedy.

**Whether you think you're wrong or think you're right—
you're right.**

Expectations can become reality. One's mind-set can become a set of blinders. While it's unlikely I'll win the big money giveaway just because I think/hope/have deluded myself into believing Publishers Clearinghouse is on the other end of the line, expecting disaster around every corner increases my chances of finding it.

102

When you find yourself sliding into that familiar negative frame of mind—STOP! *Break* that negative thinking by consciously, *forcefully* telling yourself to stop.

Research has shown that our ability to recall thoughts of one mind-set correlates to the mind-set we are in. If we are sad or unhappy, we can much more easily recall unhappy events. The ability to recall events of a particular event matches the degree of that mood we're in. Are you *really* unhappy? You'll find it *really* easy to recall unhappy moments in your life.

That's why *thought stopping* is so important to *getting control by letting go*. At this stage in the process of getting back on track it may be asking too much to be happy. But it *is* important to try to stop being sad. This is not to say you aren't entitled to your grief, sadness, melancholy over the crisis in your life. But you cannot let that emotion take over.

That's easier said than done, I know! It's been more than five years since I left the *Today* show. And yet, even today arrows from that episode seem to continue to fly in my direction. When Bryant Gumbel was preparing to leave *Today,* I was asked by Oprah Winfrey's producers to contribute a few words to a show she did in tribute to Bryant.

I was happy to oblige and spoke of Bryant's preparedness and how much I learned from him during our time together. I also joked about a Christmas gift he'd once given me: a magnifying glass for all the scrutiny I'd be under. Boy! Was he ever right about that! A few days after the taping, Bryant sent a lovely note to me thanking me for my kind words. I'd long since buried any hurt feelings I'd had and was glad to see that Bryant had, too.

So what do the papers talk about when NBC holds a farewell broadcast? The fact that Deborah Norville wasn't invited. I knew nothing about a tribute show and wouldn't have expected to be included. But I didn't expect to read the executive producer's remarks that my presence would bring back memories of a rocky period in the show's history.

The comment stung. One viewer in Texas shared with me a

copy of a letter she'd sent NBC telling them to "stop punishing Deborah Norville." I found myself starting to slide back into the old melancholy. *That's* when I resorted to thought stopping.

I told myself, "You have put this behind you. It doesn't matter what they say, so don't read it." I forcibly turned my thoughts to other things, and I didn't read the TV pages for a few days, just in case there were other "pearls of wisdom" I didn't need to see. The thought stopping worked.

When you find yourself sliding into depressive thinking—STOP! You may have to actually pinch yourself—hard—to break the thought process. (That really soft area inside your arm by your elbow is a good place to grab. Youch!) Do *not* allow yourself to return to whatever was making you feel unhappy.

Early on, it may be helpful to have an alternative happy thought to focus on. Perhaps a Bible verse or a bit of poetry is a good distraction. My favorite Bible verse is "I can do all things through Him who strengthens me" (Philippians 4:13). The Serenity Prayer is another one I like:

> God grant me the serenity to accept the things I cannot change,
> the ability to change the things I can, and the wisdom to know
> the difference.

Throughout this book, I have sprinkled quotes which have had special meaning to me as I've journeyed back from my crisis. Write down any that seem to speak to you and repeat them to yourself when you find negative thinking invading your day.

Get control by letting go. When crisis hits, one's strongest impulse is to hide. Find a cave. Hibernate until it goes away. In real life, that's not possible. Go over your daily calendar and see which tasks, chores, and people you can eliminate from your day. Clear the decks and take care of you. You deserve it.

Chapter Five

REACHING OUT

"Healing is a matter of time, but it is sometimes also a matter of opportunity."

—Hippocrates

Iᴛ ʜᴀᴅ ʙᴇᴇɴ ᴀ ʟᴏɴɢ time since Leah and I had had a chance to sit quietly and just have a cup of coffee and visit. Hard to believe, but it has now been more than fifteen years since we were roommates in college. Back then we were both journalism students, both hoping we were doing the right thing while we were in college to help ensure our chances of getting a job when we got out.

Ours was a typical college closeness. She'd helped me sort out a few boyfriend messes and I'd commiserated with her when Mr. Wonderful turned out not to be. Together we pored through the help-wanted ads in the trades and wondered, "What would it be like to live in Cedar Rapids?" When she got a "real" reporting job after graduating, she clued me in on everything about "real life," from meeting a daily news deadline to combating the cockroaches in her first tiny apartment.

Somehow, life had gotten in our way over the years. Various jobs in various parts of the country. Husbands, career changes, and finally, kids. I often thought of Leah and longed to talk with her, but the only time the opportunity to call seemed to be there was in the wee hours of the morning.

When we finally ended back in the same city, our friendship was grounded in those wonderful college years and nurtured with a periodic cup of coffee.

After sharing the stories of our boys—we both ended up with two sons—and catching up on job and husband news, I told Leah about my book. I was thrilled by her enthusiasm and told her about the real starting point for what you're reading now. I recalled for her the day I couldn't eat. The day when Niki was a little baby and I couldn't nurse him. And I retold to her the story of my promise to myself that morning when I was crying in the shower. The promise that "they" would never have that kind of control over me again.

Her eyes filled with tears and she reached across the banquette. Shaking her head, she said, "I'm so sorry," and gave me a big hug. "I didn't know you were going through that," she said as she gave me another squeeze.

Almost five years after that lonely day in the shower, Leah's hug felt awfully good.

"Trouble is part of your life. If you don't share it, you don't give the person who loves you the chance to love you enough."

—Dinah Shore

Leah couldn't have known what I was going through, because I didn't give her a chance to know. I had cloistered myself in my apartment. The only mail that went out were the bills that had to be paid. I picked up the phone only when it rang. And it didn't ring very often.

When my world fell apart, very few people called and asked me if they could help pick up the pieces. And I never reached out and asked anyone to come over with a dustpan and broom to help me sweep up the debris of my life.

I wish I'd seen then the quote I've shared above from Dinah Shore. In 20/20 hindsight, I should have picked up the phone or written notes to those friends, like Leah, who I know would have wanted to be there for me.

So many times, I've run into people like the husband of an old friend from Georgia, who when I met him said he'd followed the *Today* show saga, knowing that his wife and I were friends. "We really felt for you," he'd said. But they never called.

Or the time I ran into an old colleague from Chicago at a swanky journalists event at the Waldorf-Astoria in New York City. "Gee, Deb," she said when we hugged hello. "You look great. I felt so badly for you when you were at NBC. I meant to call you . . ." her voice trailed off. "I just didn't know what to say."

And as I did every other time I'd heard someone say something similar, I thought, "Well, I wish you would have. I could have used a friend."

"Victory finds a hundred fathers but defeat is an orphan."

—Count Galeazzo Ciano

It's easy to understand why my phone didn't ring. We live in a country that prides itself on power and triumph. We've conquered most diseases. We've won most of the wars. We've set up the democratic model for the rest of the world. The American ideal is "can do," "take no prisoners," "no holds barred." Our collective image of ourselves as a nation and as individuals is one of strength, invincibility, success.

The person in the throes of a crisis is none of these things. She is weak, vulnerable, a failure. She is not likely to reach out and make her failure even more apparent by saying, "I need to talk with you."

Instead, she becomes an actress. She plays hurt. She acts like nothing's wrong. That's also the American way. She "rises above" her injuries and stays in the game—aching all the while on the inside.

That was the way Joan Esposito behaved after her husband's suicide. "I knew how to act appropriate and act sane and act okay. And that's what I did. I was *playing* the part that I had previously lived." Joan says her act was part show for the rest of the world and part hope for the future. "I was hopeful that if you start doing it and acting it and pretending it, that sooner or later you find out it's second-nature. That's kind of how I regained my sanity."

Other women will handle their crisis as I did—withdrawing from the rest of the world as much as is remotely possible.

Perhaps you're reading and taking exception to this. "Oh no! That's not me at all!" Maybe you're *not* averse to spending time with a loser (after all, ours is also a nation of compassion). But what would you say to her?

Ah ha! There's the rub. What on earth can you say, can *anyone* say to the person whose life map has just been turned to ashes? Could anyone have made my job reappear? Could anyone have erased the label "damaged goods" from the Deborah Norville database? Of course not.

"I was lucky because my friends just flocked around me. Two or three friends called every day just to check on me. And one friend at work would come into my office and say, 'Okay—where are you today?'"

In one sense the end of Robin's marriage after thirteen years was a huge shock. In another, she'd been expecting it for a long time. For longer than she cared to remember their relationship had been based "on children and finances," as her husband, Don, put it.

"Maybe that's what happens when people begin to drift apart. I think I was willing to stay with it and keep trying. But he said he just wasn't happy. He told me, 'You don't love me the way you used to—or you would be able to do for me what I need. You *used* to do it.'

"At the time this made no sense to me at all. I said, 'How can you say that when you are the love of my life and our whole life is centered around you?'"

As best as Robin can figure, the problem seems to be Don's sense that since their two children were born, he has fallen off the list of priorities. "He'd say, 'You're creating this image of the perfect wife, the perfect mother, the perfect family—you're doing it for you. You're not doing it for me.'"

Don's resentment over time not spent with him had been building for a while. Looking back, Robin says, "I can see if you believe that the person wasn't doing the right things for you, you get angry and the anger grows a little each day for years. I think he began to say, 'It's the children who come first.'"

Robin was aware of none of this until Don broke the news that he wasn't happy and was planning to leave. It was the way he worded his feelings that hit hardest.

"I hit rock bottom the day he said, 'I will do things for you as long as it doesn't get in the way of what I need.' And I thought, *This* is *not* the man I have known for all these years!'"

Robin was lucky in that her friends rallied 'round her. Their mere presence and frequent phone calls were of great comfort. She can't recall any of them saying the wrong thing. That too puts Robin in a special group of women beset by crisis.

"I just didn't know what to say."

It's what is usually said by way of apology when someone bumps into a person they know they've let down. Translated it means, "I'm uncomfortable talking to you because I can't change what's happened." Okay. That makes sense. It *is* hard talking to someone who's going through tough times. But let's do a little comparison here: who's more uncomfortable? The gal whose life has fallen into a thousand little pieces—or the guy who's got to talk to her? You get my point.

But the reality is—once the initial crisis has passed, you're very likely to find yourself *alone* with your thoughts and your problems—unless *you* reach out.

When Joan lost her husband to suicide, she found herself surrounded by co-workers and family and friends. Everyone she needed rallied 'round to support her.

Losing a husband under any circumstances is awful. But Joan's situation was tragic. Married less than a year, the news that Joan, at age thirty-nine, was expecting their first child only underscored her belief that *finally* everything in her life was coming together. The knowledge that a baby was on the way was the final brush stroke to the beautiful painting that had become her life.

Bryan's death instantly turned the canvas black.

Her friends got her through it. "My family and my friends just kept me on my feet when I could not have done it alone. And they held me up until I could walk on my own."

Joan says it wasn't that anyone said anything particularly inspirational during those first traumatic days. In a situation like suicide, she says, there really *is* nothing one can say. "I think no matter what the crisis, the best thing is to say 'I'm sorry and I love you and I really think you're terrific!' and leave it at that."

That's why STEP FOUR TO GETTING BACK ON TRACK is so important: REACH OUT TO OTHERS

Let those who love you have a chance to love you enough. Thucydides said, "We secure our friends not by accepting favors, but by doing them." Let your friends solidify their relationship with you by allowing them to be *there* for you. They can only do this—if you *let them know you need them!*

It's not only a healthy thing for your friendship. It is also a good thing for your body.

Isolation can be deadly. We've all read the articles about the health dangers of smoking, high blood pressure, high cholesterol, and lack of exercise. Isolation is worse than all of these.

Being alone, cutting yourself off from normal social interaction, can have devastating effects on your health. Isolation is reported to *double* the chance of sickness or death. *Double!* Studies show that while smoking increases mortality by a risk factor of 1.6, isolation increases the risk by 2.0.

A study done at Mount Sinai School of Medicine in New York sheds even more light on the negatives of being alone. Doctors monitored husbands of women who were in the advanced stages of breast cancer. The men gave blood samples every six to eight weeks during their wives' illnesses—and for up to fourteen months after the women died.

The stress of caring for an ill spouse and watching a loved one die did not appear to impact adversely on the husbands' health. None of them showed any weakening of their immune system. But after the women passed away—in some cases, as soon as two weeks after—the surviving spouses showed signs of depressed immune function. The researchers concluded it may be bereavement—being left alone—that gave rise to more illnesses.

Another study done at Santa Clara University reaches similar conclusions by finding that people who keep painful secrets to themselves not only suffer more anxiety and depression, but physical ailments as well. They are more prone to headaches, indigestion, and fatigue. Having the emotional support of outside contacts may act as something of an insurance policy against illness.

Maybe you won't break out of your cocoon to improve your mental health. Perhaps the thought of dying is a better motivator. Whatever the motivation, now that you've decided you could use the help of a friend—how do you get word around to those who could help you?

There are a number of ways.

Most of us have a friend or acquaintance whose name is the one that gets filled in on the old joke: "Tel-e-phone, Tel-e-graph, Tell: so and so." Let gossip work *for* you. If you've got someone in your circle with a kind heart but a big mouth, I'd suggest you contact them first.

If you don't have a kindly motormouth, then take out your address book or Christmas card list and write down the names, addresses, and phone numbers of four people. Choose people *you* would want to call *you* if they were having a crisis.

As I said before, I don't consider the telephone a friend. I think it all stems from randomly dialing numbers on the phone when I was a kid and getting a callback from a very angry and very official-sounding telephone operator! To this day, I just hate to pick up the phone. I'm always convinced I'm inconveniencing the person I ring up.

If that's also your situation or if (more likely) you're reluctant to face rejection "up close and personal" on the telephone, then write your four friends.

"I need you."

Your message is simple. Just say the truth. If Jana were writing while convalescing after her automobile accident, her letter might have read, "I'm still stuck in the hospital and I'm scared to death of what it will be like when they let me leave. They say I may never walk again. What will I do? I know you don't have the answer to that—I guess no one does—but I sure would like to hear from you."

My own letter might have gone something like this: "Just thought I'd write and say hi! It's been pretty tough lately with round-the-clock feedings and all the negotiations with work.

"(name deleted to protect the guilty!) said he'd call me, but the phone hasn't rung. If you've got a free minute, call me. It would be nice to hear your voice."

Both of these letters hint at what's really going on in the

writer's mind, but only vaguely. Jana speaks to her fear of being fifteen and never walking again. My letter intimates that someone I would have hoped would call me didn't.

Perhaps in *your* moment of crisis, you'll be better able to ask directly for help. See if this sample letter is useful:

> Dear __,
>
> It's hard to believe but it's been (time) since (crisis) happened. I'm still trying to sort through it all and don't really know if I'll ever have what's happened to me all figured out. There are good days and there are bad days. Much more of the latter, to be honest.
>
> I know you don't have the answers either, but it would be good to hear from/talk with/meet you sometime. Do you think you could write/call/meet me? I've missed talking with you and think frankly the visit could do me some good right now. Please call anytime, I look forward to hearing from you soon.
>
> Best,

There you have it. A short, simple unmistakable request for help that you can make with minimal risk on your part. What's the worst that can happen? You don't hear back from dear so-and-so. It cost you thirty-two cents and five minutes of your time to learn that dear so-and-so is wasting valuable space in your address book. Unless they've got a *very* good reason for ignoring your plea, you needn't think about them again.

That's part of the reason you're going to send out four letters at a time. And why you're going to send four the next week and the week after that.

The point is not that you've got to send out a dozen letters to get a response. But rather, you need the support of a variety of friends during this tough period. Your letter-writing campaign is going to help bring them into the fold.

"I don't think I ever even considered what I would do if I had a cri-

113

sis. I don't dwell on the negative or the 'what if?' I'd rather think in terms of what's happening now is good. It's great and how can I make it better?"

With her sunny disposition, Christina is the picture of optimism and achievement. She and her husband have a solid marriage and an energetic five-year-old son who is the light of their lives. They've worked hard for their home and their future looks secure.

But over the past four years, Christina has had to struggle through a series of miscarriages, each one more painful than the one before.

"The first time, it was 'Well, I didn't know *this* could happen to me!'" Christina is matter-of-fact when she starts to share her story. "I figured I fell into what I considered to be a small percentage of just bad luck. Then I got pregnant again and this time it was twins. And the same thing happened again that happened two or three months previously."

About nine or ten weeks into her pregnancy, Christina miscarried one of the twins. Determined to bring the second twin to term, she took to her bed and followed the doctor's orders to the letter. But six months into her pregnancy—twenty-three weeks and one day after she'd conceived—Christina went into labor and lost that baby, a boy, as well. It was a devastating loss that left her spinning.

"I thought, 'This is crazy,'" she recalls. "I've done what I was supposed to do. This is *not* supposed to happen." Christina stopped and seemed to be lost in her memories before she resumed her matter-of-fact voice. "Then you get to the point where you say, 'Well, I guess there really is nothing I could have done differently.'"

For Christina, reaching out to others was essential in helping her cope with the grief over this third miscarriage. She wrote letters to all the hospital staff who'd attended her and the baby, thanking them for their efforts on her behalf.

"It was for me a way of trying to have some kind of closure on the whole event." The other step she took to try to cope with her sadness was to start a diary.

"In terms of my miscarriages, I didn't write a sentence after the first two. But after the third I got an inexpensive plain page diary and wrote down everything that happened from the time we lost the first twin and onward."

Her diary is a poignant yet dignified recounting of that sad night. In her even script, Christina describes how she jokingly asked her husband if it was a full moon, the baby was moving so much. Later, in the middle of the night, she was timing contractions and by three o'clock in the morning, Christina and her husband were at the hospital. She was in labor. It was a Sunday.

"My husband is what got me through the entire ordeal," she writes. *"I held his hand the entire time . . . he gave me the strength and calmness I needed to keep from panicking."* Later, after the baby was delivered and declared dead, she became philosophical: *"That night and during the night we experienced such a closeness, peace even, knowing that the Lord had blessed us in taking our small child home to be with him on a Sunday. . . .*

"Our sweet Jonathan, almost two and a half years old, will not have to experience watching a brother who can't run fast or do the same things he can do."

The next day: *"It seems every time I shut my eyes, the whole delivery comes back."* By the time a week had passed, Christina's writings hint at the beginnings of a lessening of the pain: *"Jonathan often comes up to tell me he loves me BERRY MUCH! I am truly blessed!"*

Christina says her diary not only gave her a release for her pain upon losing her baby, but was tangible proof later on of just how much of a recovery she'd made.

Two and a half years later, Christina and her husband tried one more time to have a child—this time after innumerable visits to specialists in two states. She conceived, but it was not to be. Again, about two and a half months into her pregnancy, Christina had the now familiar spotting followed by cramping. This time, she didn't need a doctor to tell her—this baby would not make it either.

Christina went off the deep end.

"I didn't want to see anybody, I didn't want to talk to anybody. I unplugged the answering machine. I turned the ringers off the phone. I went to my room. I didn't want to watch TV. I just lay there.

"I cried until you just can't cry anymore. You're exhausted. Your eyes are puffy and you get to where you can't breathe from crying so much."

"Would it have made a difference if someone had sent you a little note on that day?" I asked. "Something like, 'I'm thinking about you?'"

"Oh I definitely think so." Christina was absolute in her answer. "If I had gotten a card like that on *that* day, it definitely would have had a much greater impact than the same card a week earlier or a week later."

"Apt words have power to suage the tumors of a troubled mind."

—John Milton

Unfortunately, your letter-writing campaign will not help your well-intentioned friends say the right things. What *not* to say? Joan is emphatic on this point: "Relating an anecdote of your own pain doesn't help. You don't want to hear, 'Well, my cousin committed suicide . . .' Big fucking deal! Who gives a shit! All *you* know is you are hurting big-time and you need someone to say I'm sorry you're hurting and give them a mental hug or a physical hug. *That's* the best thing to do for anybody."

Think of some of the "kindhearted" remarks you might have heard or perhaps have shared yourself in the past:

"It's not the end of the world."
"After all, you've got a healthy baby to take care of."
"You're strong, you'll get through it."
"God never gives you more than you can handle."

Intellectually, each one of those statements is correct. But the person who's on the receiving end is not thinking intellectually. In a crisis, your emotional side takes over—rightly or wrongly. You are not necessarily thinking rationally. And the emotional filter through which these well-intentioned statements must travel can cause quite a change during the translation.

EXAMPLE: "It's not the end of the world."
Well, of course it isn't, stupid. If this were the end of the world, the walls would be crashing right about now and you'd probably be doing something a little more productive than throwing platitudes my way. (No one said a person in the midst of a crisis is a shrinking violet!)

The "end of the world" statement is more likely received by the person in crisis as *really* saying, "What are you complaining about. You're still alive/walking/employed, etc." At the moment of crisis, being alive/walking/employed, etc. isn't necessarily something to cheer about.

EXAMPLE: "After all, you've got a healthy baby to take care of."
Indeed, the woman in crisis does have a child or children at home who call her Mommy. The statement is true. But the translated meaning behind it is cuttingly cruel: "That miscarriage wasn't really a baby. There isn't anything to mourn here. Forget about that baby you lost."

EXAMPLE: "You're strong, you'll get through it."
Yes, the fact is there isn't much in life we *don't* get through. But when the "you're strong" statement is presented to the woman in crisis, what's heard isn't "I've got faith in you and I know you'll come through this" but rather "I really don't want to be bothered by you. Take care of yourself."

EXAMPLE: "God never gives you more than you can handle."
This is a religious variation on the "you're strong" platitude. I'll confess, I'm particularly guilty of passing this one around. My intention is that it be interpreted as the "God will help you get through this if you'll let your faith rely on Him." It is more likely being heard, however, as, "How dare you complain about anything! You're going against God if you gripe about the lot you've been given."

None of those hidden messages are what the well-intentioned individual wanted their friend to hear. But the woman in crisis looks at the world through black glasses.

So what works? If the standard lines we've always relied upon to help those we care about during their times of need really cause more problems then they solve, what *can* we say?

We can say what we feel. Honestly. And from the heart.

Could anyone make Joan's husband come back from the grave? Could anyone really explain *why* he'd taken his own life? Of course not. And Joan knew that.

What might have been nice to hear would have been, "I've racked my brain and I can't think of why it all happened." Or an honest, "I hope that someday all of this makes sense. I'm praying for you." Even a frank, "Man, if Bryan were here, I'd punch him in the nose for putting you through all of this!"

The comments that help best are those which validate what the sufferer is feeling. Was Joan angry at her husband for choosing to die? You bet! It's a common response for suicide survivors. The "punch his nose" remark strikes right at the heart of her anger and provides an opportunity for a good chuckle.

The "I don't know why" and "I hope it someday makes sense" comments are a subtle, supportive way of saying "Yes, it *is* confusing and even though I'm thinking clearly, I can't figure it out either."

Sometimes the simplest remark can be the most helpful:

"I'm so sorry."
or
"Do you want to talk about it?"
or
"This must be so painful."
or
"I love you."

Since we *do* live in a society in which displays of frailty and weakness are frowned upon, those four simple lines can help open a door that the woman in crisis might be unwilling to open voluntarily. Perhaps she's been holding in a raft of thoughts and feelings that you can allow her to pour out to you. Maybe not. But you've given her an opening that she can use *if it's right for her at this time*.

This leads to the inevitable question of therapy. I can't speak to this from personal experience. Millions of people have benefited from working with a professional therapist. I suppose I'm a bit of a skeptic.

Obviously my advice to reach out to friends and share with them is based upon the notion that sharing one's thoughts and fears, "spilling your guts" as it were, can be cathartic. As you'll see later on in this chapter, I have a number of specific written exercises which are rooted in this theory. A professional certainly knows the right questions to ask to more quickly get to the *real fears* that are at the heart of the angst that's kept an individual from moving beyond her crisis.

In Marcia's case, only a professional rape counselor could help her sort through the tangled emotions and fears that crippled her after her attack. It was her boyfriend, Bill, who'd stayed by her side throughout the ordeal who finally persuaded her to see a professional.

"So many of the issues that follow a rape are dealing with your closest friends and associates and dealing with physical intimacy. In my case, the rapist was claiming to want to give me pleasure and that had tremendous implications for future lovemaking. How could my boyfriend pay me a compliment or try to give me pleasure and not have it harken back to such pain? That was a big part of my rape."

Marcia's counselor helped her put her rape in a context she'd not considered before. She was, in fact, extremely fortunate. "I mean, this person could have decided to pick up whatever I saw shine in the light and ended my life forever. He could have mutilated me." Marcia pauses as that thought sinks in. "He could have ended my life forever. I was lucky to be alive."

It is clear that only a professional could have helped Marcia sort through her pain and exorcise her dark thoughts. There are some specific crises for which it is probably best to seek professional advice. In the Resources section you'll find some telephone numbers that should be of some help.

When Robin was separated from her husband, she sought the advice of a therapist who was helpful in making her realize that what were issues in the failure of her marriage were not just failings on her part.

"Don kept saying, 'Your body used to be so pretty. You let it go to pot.' He said I never smelled good enough. I was never sexy enough. Why don't you do this or why don't you do that?" Robin took Don's criticisms to heart because she believed him. She'd hung on his every word for more than a decade, including the critical ones.

She says her therapist helped her see the comments from a different vantage point. "The therapist says, 'So *he* has this obsession with me not smelling good. That's *his* hang-up.'" With amazement Robin exclaims, "You know—I had never seen it that way!"

Chances are Robin would have come to these realizations on her own. The therapist helped her see it more quickly. And the real value of therapy to Robin was that this was something she was doing for herself. The fee she spent on her sessions and the time she reserved to keep her appointments were a selfish acknowledgment on her part that she was *worth* it. That she was important enough for precious time and money to be spent—not wasted—on her. After putting children and husband and jobs first, this was a monumental step.

But for that general malaise, the nonspecific down-in-the-dumps kind of trouble, I must confess I am a bit of a skeptic about professionals. I know many people swear by therapy and, on one hand, I really can't blame them. After all, who wouldn't rave about forty-five minutes or an hour of uninterrupted time when she's the center of attention? How many of us wouldn't wax enthusiastic about such a space of time during which every thought and utterance is made with ourselves in mind?

How many times does that happen in any grown woman's life? I can think of a couple of center-of-attention moments: my wedding day, my baby showers, and the moment I walked into the hospital to deliver each of my two sons. In each of those situations, *I* was the star attraction. The wedding pictures were about the BRIDE—and *then* the rest of the people. Those baby presents were for ME to open and get excited about. No one expected Karl to ooh and aah over the nighttime bottle warmer—and he didn't.

And those hospital aides couldn't move fast enough when I arrived at New York Hospital to have my babies. (Mind you, it didn't last past the birth. Once that baby arrives, mom is nothing more than the mode of transportation and the feed mule!)

No. There is no question about it—being front and center *is* awfully nice. And for $75 an hour—or whatever the going rate is in your community—you can be front and center at your therapist's.

My concern about therapy is the potential for trading one crutch—in this case the crisis that brought you here—for another: the security of that weekly appointment. We've all heard of people who've been in therapy for years. Why? If after a certain point, you're just not much further down the road toward feeling strong again, maybe this kind of therapy isn't the answer for you.

121

And who's more likely to say it's time to stop this exercise? Do you really expect the therapist to one day open a session with, "Mrs. Smith, you've been coming here for three years on a weekly basis and you've made great strides. But I really don't think I can be of much more assistance to you. This will be our last session."

Sure! Yeah! Right.

I've no doubt that 99.9 percent of those who've chosen to work in the field of therapy are concerned men and women who want the best for their clients. But therapists *are* men and women. They're human. Just as Mrs. Smith has come to expect that Thursday morning appointment and look forward to it, Mrs. Smith has also become a part of the therapist's weekly routine—*AND* an important part of the therapist's bottom line.

If Mrs. Smith isn't there on Thursday, who will fill that space in the appointment book? That blank space means lost income. Maybe Mrs. Smith *has* stopped making great strides therapeutically. But her checks haven't stopped clearing and that has got to make those stalemated sessions a bit easier for our professional to swallow.

I don't discount therapy. But you might give some homemade therapy a try first. Let your friends minister to you with their own good common sense and their advice born of genuine love and concern for you. If you honestly think, "No, Deborah, you're wrong. I need the advice of an expert," I can't argue with you. Maybe you do. But do me a favor. Read through the rest of this book (especially the part on "experts" in Chapter 8). My hope is, by the time you've read all the way to the end you will feel strong and confident in yourself. But just in case you need some outside assistance, you'll find some places to start your search in the Resource section.

"The only thing that endures is change."

—Albert Camus

What are you most afraid of? When you look at the changes that this crisis has brought to your life, which ones are so terrifying that you find yourself chasing those images right out of your mind?

Let's grab those fears and wrestle them away! "Bonx them in the noodle" as Niki would say. Or if you prefer a more erudite description, to paraphrase former presidential hopeful Steve Forbes, let's take those fears and "Kill 'em, choke 'em, drive a stake through their hearts" so they can never rise up again to bother you.

Take a notebook. I prefer those 5 × 7 side-spiral-bound notebooks you find in the school supply section at the grocery store. Flip past the first few pages and start a page with the heading: FEARS.

Guess what I want you to write down? Um, hmm. Everything you are afraid of. *Everything!* I don't care how stupid, unlikely, insignificant, earth-shattering, or implausible those fears are. I want you to write them down.

Make sure you tackle this task at a time when you'll be able to think without interruption. Do this when you won't have to keep handy that brave face you've been showing the rest of the world. To come up with *all* of your fears, you will have to dig deep into some dark recesses of your imagination. It won't be easy. It won't necessarily be fun. And you *won't* particularly enjoy this. But hang in there. Do the best you can. There's a method to this madness.

When I left *Today,* my fear list seemed endless. I was worried about everything. I was worried about the amount of time I spent worrying. And I was afraid that I would never *stop* worrying. It was a maddening swirl that seemed to suck me in like bathwater whirlpooling down the drain. I was consumed by my fears.

And what was I afraid of? You name it.

I was afraid I would never work in television again. Actually that wasn't really a fear as much as a very depressing certainty to me.

I was afraid that without my work, Karl wouldn't love me. After all, reporting the news had been my life since long before my husband and I had met—how could I possibly be as interesting and aware of the world if I wasn't up to my elbows in wire copy? Maybe preparing for interviews was what made me attractive to

123

him? Without the stimulation of the newsroom, maybe I was the ultimate stick-in-the-mud.

He'd always said he was attracted to me because I was smart. But, I worried, was it my work that made me seem smart? What if he now found me boring and left me for more exciting pastures?

I was afraid financially too. We had been blessed economically. But if I didn't work, would our fortunes change? As a child, my mother had always said to my sisters and me, "I never want you to be dependent upon a man for your survival."

"Oh no!" I thought over and again. "If I can't get a job I'll have to be dependent on Karl, and maybe he'll walk out on me and maybe I'll have no place to live and what will we eat and . . ."

The thoughts whirled faster and faster, each fear playing off the one before it. Each fear becoming more and more unrealistic.

And that's the point in writing your fears down. When your worries and concerns are flying around in your imagination they seem realistic and believable. On paper, they appear as ridiculous as most of us looked in our prom pictures. Your mind's eye is a prism that skews reality. The harsh truth of words on paper cuts through the illusion. It makes the absurd fears apparent in their preposterousness.

Put these fears on paper, and then wait a couple of days and go back over them when you're feeling stronger. How many of those concerns that seemed so legitimate when you wrote them down, now seem foolish? Are your fears *rational?*

When I now go back over my own fears at the time of my crisis, I see how clouded my thinking was by emotion. Of all the worries I had, the only one that truly seems realistic was the first: I might not ever work in my chosen field again.

- My husband was not the sort to desert during disaster.
- I was not likely to become a mush brain just because I wasn't doing daily interviews on the day's events.
- I've been saving for retirement since I was twenty-three—bankruptcy was not looming on my horizon.

- If for some reason I *did* become homeless, was it possible for even an instant that my dad and three sisters in Georgia wouldn't come to my rescue?

Of course not.

Writing down your fears allows you to put some distance between yourself and your concerns and *confront* them. The separation created by putting these naturally frightening feelings on paper makes it easier to see them in a broader context.

Jana Stump put some of her deepest and most troubling thoughts on paper. Now six years after her accident, she has found that her journal not only gives her a benchmark against which to measure her progress, it also has been a place to share the thoughts that at the time she could share with no one else. During that difficult first year when she was trying to transition back to high school as the town's only wheelchair-bound student, she poured her anger onto the pages of her journal.

February 2, 1991 was a very tough day for her:

I find myself with my plastered fake enamel look. I pretend to smile, pretend to live. I've hung on for a good eight and a half months. Don't even think I haven't given myself a chance. . . .

Now I think about death, how ugly I am. I wish the basketball team would get dunked—literally. Stabbing my little sister's brains in the garbage disposal, throwing a dart at my dad's vocal chords, and just drug up my mother.

If I knew a psychiatrist I would go in a second. I'm admitting—I need serious help.

Hateful and frightening as these thoughts were, putting them on paper gave Jana a place where she could deal with them. Committing her feelings to paper took some of the sting out of them. And years later, she has a very clear indicator of just how well she's gotten back on track.

There is an ancillary health benefit in this exercise. In a study done at Southern Methodist University, researchers found that talking about their troubles was not only an emotional solace for people, but medically beneficial as well. Dr. James Pennebaker had participants spend fifteen minutes a day for five days writing about their troubles. His team then medically evaluated the participants and found enhanced immune function, fewer trips to the doctor, fewer days of missed work, and improved liver enzyme function. These were private thoughts put simply on paper.

While such physical benefits are nice to hear about, to me it's really just icing on the cake. The real point of putting your fears on paper is to allow you to move outside your worries.

Viewed critically, some of your fears *will* seem absurdly unrealistic. And others will be right on target. Having those fears on paper, knowing what troubles you really *do* have to deal with will make it easier for you to prioritize your future and take those *best steps* to get your life back on track and put the current crisis behind you.

This is the beginning of your life road map. As Scarlett said, "After all, tomorrow is another day." This road map you're going to write will help you get there . . . and make sure that *your* tomorrow is bright and sunny.

Chapter Six

WHAT ABOUT ME?

"Too much of a good thing can be wonderful."
—Mae West

FOR OVER A YEAR AFTER her husband walked out, Robin had been waiting for "feeling" to return. In a way, she was still in shock. She still couldn't believe that Don was gone. For a year, she'd been trying to understand his announcement that he wasn't happy. Though she'd had time to adjust to the idea, it seemed to her that leaving after thirteen years of marriage, two kids, and the struggle of building a life together just made no sense.

"He says he feels left out," a perplexed Robin explains. "That since the kids came, he didn't matter anymore. That's it. There's not another woman, we haven't had huge fights—I guess he's having a midlife crisis."

Robin was at a loss to explain *why* her marriage had collapsed. And at this point, she really didn't care. Fourteen months of trying to figure it out had left her exhausted. They'd tried therapy. That didn't work. Don and the therapist had ended up at odds, leaving Robin in even more despair because she realized Don was putting no real effort into the therapy—he was just going through the motions.

In the beginning Robin tried to patch things together. But no matter what she tried—spending more time with him, involving him more with the children, being more sexy, planning evenings for just the two of them—Don was unresponsive.

He moved out. First he was gone just a couple nights a week. Then he'd set up separate housekeeping altogether. Now there were lawyers involved.

Today was not a day she expected to go well. It was her son's birthday. She'd been dreading today because she knew it meant she and Don would be together *a lot*. She agonized over what to wear. "I don't want him to be able to look at me and see how badly I've been hurting," she shared. "And I want him to eat his heart out!"

Robin had lost a good fifteen pounds since Don left. She'd never been heavy, but she now weighed what she did when she and Don met fifteen years ago. Those skintight leggings that usually made her feel fat now looked like a million bucks. She put on the leggings and headed off to the party.

The birthday was to be held at a local arts and crafts shop. Fifteen eight-year-olds had descended upon the ceramics studio where they were given a choice of preformed objects to turn into glazed "works of art."

It was just the kind of activity an eight-year-old could get into. Paint, brushes, and no one yelling about the mess they were making. Within minutes, the kids began to cover their cars and boxes with color and the room hummed with activity. Once Robin got the kids directed, she decided to give it a try. Walking over to the shelf, she chose a large sombrero with a hollow top. It had great potential for chips and dip.

It had been years since Robin had attempted anything more artistically ambitious than sketching pictures for the kids to color. And yet she became engrossed in decorating the dish for glazing. The room was alive with the noise of the children and their parents, yet in the middle of the mayhem Robin felt as though she'd been transported to an oasis of serenity.

"You should have seen me," she said later that day. "I was finding all these great colors. I painted the hat red and I used a really small brush to do the rope trim in black and gold."

Robin's excitement about her creative effort was evident. "I couldn't believe what fun it was! I told the kids as soon as the dish gets glazed, we'd fill it up with nachos and dip and have a big party."

There was more energy in Robin's voice than there had been for months.

"I can't believe I'm making such a big deal of such a stupid bowl!" she laughed. "But I'll admit it, I had a great time!"

On the day that Robin predicted her breakup would take its greatest toll, she felt better than she had in ages. During that brief time that she was focused on her project, she forgot her pain. That absence of pain reminded her what it felt like to feel good.

The woman's work that is never done is probably what she asked her husband to do.

Like two thirds of American women with children under age thirteen, Robin is a working mother. With a divorce pending, she's now grateful for her job—but she wonders if the combined demands of job and children and household didn't help widen the gap between her and Don.

"It's not one person's fault," she explains. "It's both of you contributing to this."

I asked Robin if she could point to a wrong turn that she and Don had taken. She explained that it was more of a curve in the road than a finite turn. "You've got a lot of demands and so something has to give. You have the children and you both fall so madly, crazily, passionately in love with these children. And they become everything. And then in the process, you neglect the two of you."

Looking at Robin and Don's marriage, they probably made more of an effort at their relationship than many couples. About seven years into the marriage, Don suggested they reserve just one night a week for themselves. Their children were quite small at the time. Friday night, it was decided, would be date night.

"We did it for a little while. On Friday nights, we'd stay home and have champagne and chocolates. We'd shut the door to our room for 'our night.'" Robin stopped to run her hand through her hair. "Somewhere along the line, we stopped doing that. I think now, 'How much of that was my fault? How much was his fault?'"

It's little wonder time together was limited. It's been reported that the average working mother in America spends more than eighty hours per week on all her "jobs"—both paid and unpaid. I personally think that figure is way on the low side.

As we saw in Chapter 2, today's women *do* wear many hats. Now I'm going to ask you to wear one more: the selfish "me" hat.

STEP FIVE TO GETTING BACK ON TRACK: DO SOMETHING FOR YOURSELF

When is the last time you had a facial or a massage? Or more likely, have you *ever* had a facial or massage? When I asked Robin that question, I was astonished at her answer: she had *never* had a facial. This attractive, successful, impeccably groomed woman had never in her forty-plus years treated herself to the luxury of a facial!

When is the last time you took a nap? Is the answer really that there just isn't time, or is it more likely, you're not *taking* the time? I'll bet you can easily think of ten reasons why you can't take a little time for yourself. The kids need watching. There's laundry to be done. I've got a report due at the office. It's tax time and I've got to wade through the papers. Dinner's got to get started.

I think it is our nature as women to often put on the hair shirt and think to ourselves, "It is my lot as a female to suffer." And it's true a lot of *tsuris* does come our way. But ignoring yourself is a good way to add to your problems.

It is not a badge of honor to ignore yourself.

What are you really saying when you say, I don't have time for a nap. I shouldn't spend the money on a manicure. It wouldn't be right for me to buy new makeup.

You are saying, I am not worthy. I do not matter. I don't count. You are putting yourself further into that depressive mind-set that has led to the feelings of failure and inadequacy you're currently struggling with.

Maybe you've been told by someone whose opinion matters to you that you aren't worthy. Robin's husband repeatedly told her she was ugly and not sexy. Who wouldn't feel they don't matter when their loved one batters them with a constant refrain of criticism?

Maybe you've been told you're unimportant not in words, but in action. Has it ever happened that you've told your husband something and he has absolutely no recollection of it. It has to me—on more than one occasion! Recently I was being honored by the local Junior League as a Woman of Achievement. I was really excited about being selected because to me the Junior League Ladies were always the epitome of grace and community service. I told my husband of my selection and gave him the date of the event.

What happened? He scheduled a business trip for that night to Atlanta.

"But honey," I whined when we went over our schedules. "That's when I'm being honored by the Junior League!"

"You didn't tell me," he quickly replied.

Now I *know* that I had told him—this was a big deal to me. He just didn't hear me.

In the days before I felt I was back on track, I would have been crushed by his mistake. I would have read a number of messages into his failure to hear something I had so clearly told him (and, I'm sure, told him with such excitement).

I would have thought, "I speak and he just doesn't hear me—he doesn't think I'm important enough to listen to." I would have thought, "I speak and he automatically discounts what I'm about to say as not being worth listening to." I would have thought, "He thinks this award is a joke—even though it is important to me." "What is meaningful and exciting to me," I would have thought, "isn't even worth remembering to him."

I would have gone further and further into my little shell and ventured out less and less. I would have done badly in my acceptance remarks, knowing that my husband thinks this event is insignificant. I would think, "He's right—this is a joke, I don't deserve this." And I would have fallen further into that abyss that seemed to have swallowed me whole.

That would have been my reaction *before*. That wasn't how I handled it now at all. Instead, I felt bad that Karl was going to miss a really fun evening. I felt even more loved because a whole tableful of my girlfriends responded to the invitation to attend. And when I shared some of my story, which I've been telling you more fully here, about how I rebuilt my post-*Today* life, I spoke with gusto and enthusiasm. I know some women there were helped by hearing about my struggle.

And two days later, when Karl saw the beautiful roses they'd given me and the lovely crystal bowl, I knew he was sincere when he said, "Gee, Deb, I wish I had been there."

You *may* be getting messages, not so subtle and otherwise, that you aren't important. The messenger is wrong.

You deserve a moment or two of selfish pleasure. If *you* aren't worth it, then who is?

"There's not a minute of our lives should stretch without some pleasure now."

—Antony, in *Antony and Cleopatra,* by William Shakespeare

In the weeks and months following the Oklahoma bombing, there weren't many moments that Caye Allen could exactly call pleasurable. Caye and I had met the day after the explosion when my producers at *Inside Edition* had sent me over to the local church where victims' families had gathered for information and consolation.

"Find me some victims," had been their order. I couldn't imagine anything more vulturelike than descending on these poor individuals whose lives were in such upheaval. But in television, I guess you've got to "find some victims." So, my crew and I had driven to the furthest point in the parking lot to park the car. My hope was I'd bump into someone who might talk, thus sparing me (and the grieving families) the agony of walking up to them with mike in hand.

Caye had just parked Ted's white pickup when I walked by and said hello. To my great surprise, she was willing to talk about her missing husband. Many months after the explosion, I asked her if it wasn't awful the way the media descended on the town.

"Oh no," she protested. "It wasn't awful. To me, it gave me the opportunity to show people my husband. I didn't want him to be just the sixty-ninth or seventy-ninth victim of the 'Oklahoma Bombing.' I had the opportunity to show a lot of people that he was a wonderful husband and father and caring individual. It helped me then to talk about it and it helps me now. And, it will be like that forever."

But talking about her late husband doesn't always make it easier for Caye to handle the day-to-day routine. She's having trouble getting everything done. And it's a big source of frustration.

"I'm not organized like I was before and I can't adjust," she relates. "I just don't feel like there are enough hours in the day. Ted was a good helper and we'd take turns with things like Austin's bath and getting him ready for stuff. There isn't anybody else to help."

In her private moments, Caye acknowledges just how hard it is to be alone. "There are times when I sit down on the bed and I am so tired I can't even bend over to tie my shoe. And I'll think, 'I can't do everything, so I'm not going to do *any* of it.'" After a deep breath, she continues, "But of course, I get up and go ahead and do it."

"Do you have any time for yourself?" I asked.

"Very little," Caye replied.

"Do you feel like you need it?"

"Sometimes. Sometimes, I do. I didn't have much time for my-self before, it's just a little less time for myself now."

In fact, Caye had to go almost a year back in time to remem-ber a moment she took for herself. "I remember last summer I would go to the bathroom and sit in the tub for two hours. I would just sit there and say, 'Go away!' when they would come to the door. I would stay in there until I was all 'pruned'! But—that was my escape. It was the only place I could be by myself."

Life was made to be lived and enjoyed. As Diane Sawyer once said, "This is not a forced march." Do something for yourself. Cre-ate your own moment of pleasure and revel in it. *Allow* yourself to feel good.

Trouble is—too many of us don't know how.

In anyone's book Rebeccah has a dream life. She was born to a life of privilege, as was her husband, who frankly is a hunk. Now in her late twenties, she's an at-home mom with live-in baby-sitters to help with the children. Within weeks of her second baby's birth, she was back in size four jeans.

Her days consist of play dates with her children, decorating their new home in the most fashionable part of town, planning trips abroad with her husband and social evenings in town. And she's miserable. She doesn't particularly like herself. She is uninter-ested in everything.

"I know I shouldn't feel this way, but I just can't snap out of it," she moans. "I just don't know what to do. I'd always heard that a 'Home where the mother is not happy is not a happy home.' And our home was not a happy place because I was miserable."

It was Rebeccah's husband who helped her get turned around. He saw how despondent his wife was and encouraged her to do something for herself. He bought her a year's worth of facials at the local salon and encouraged her not only to use them, but to do some other "selfish" things.

"He encouraged me to get out of the house, even if it was for just a couple of hours. He said, 'I work out at the gym five days a week because if I didn't do something I really enjoy, I couldn't work as hard as I do.'" A year later, Rebeccah feels good about herself and has left behind the doldrums in which she was languishing.

Now Rebeccah attends an exercise class twice a week. She's made an effort to get to know some of the other moms in her son's nursery class and socialize with them. And she uses that coupon for a facial every month.

"It's not like I've abandoned the children. In fact, I actually spend more time with them—and now, I really enjoy it."

Taking a bit of time for yourself may be one of the most difficult tasks I'll suggest to you in this book. When I recommended to Robin she should selfishly do something she enjoys, her reply was so sad. "I don't know what I enjoy anymore, Deb." Her voice was flat with exhaustion. "I don't think anything will ever make me happy again. Don was my *soul* mate!"

So much of Robin's sense of who she was came from her relationship with her husband that she had lost sight of herself. A question that any child could answer, "What's your favorite thing to do?" was one that completely stumped her.

That's the hallmark of crisis. Your life's road map has been ripped to shreds. The constants in your world have been taken away. The reliable guideposts and support systems no longer exist—or we're no longer able to see them.

Crisis strips us bare. It robs us of our sense of mastery. We don't want to *do* anything because we *can't* do anything. Like the child who's afraid to try anything because they might fail at it, the woman in crisis is reluctant to try anything new. Afraid to do anything for herself.

Our journey toward getting back on track began with little baby steps. It is continuing now with the first act of a child: self-satisfaction. Just as a baby's initial concerns are only for his comfort and well-being, that is your concern now. And if, like Robin, your response to the admonition to "Do something for yourself" is "I don't know how," the following list should be a good starter.

Thirty-seven Ways to Take Care of Yourself

1. Get a pedicure
2. Get a manicure
3. Take a walk in nature
4. Get a massage
5. Take a nap
6. Give away or throw out your old shoes
7. Buy sexy panties
8. Get a haircut
9. Volunteer at the hospital
10. Give cookies to a friend
11. Eat the cookies instead!
12. Learn to embroider
13. Buy yourself a scarf
14. Have your legs waxed
15. Watch the stars in the backyard at night
16. Smear Vaseline on your feet and hands at night and cover with socks
17. Send yourself flowers two or three weeks from now and be surprised when they arrive
18. Race a child or co-worker down the hall (You'd be amazed how good you feel after a race—there's no way you can avoid giggling!)
19. Soak in the tub with fragrant oils
20. Take the local bus tour of your town
21. Attend a musical concert or great ballet
22. Get a makeover at the department store counter
23. Get a kitten
24. Work out
25. Plant flowers in the garden or window box

26. Give yourself that sweater or purse you've been longing for—or put it on layaway
27. Wash the car meticulously both inside and out
28. Take a shoebox and cover it with beautiful paper
30. Whip egg whites and give yourself a firming facial mask
31. Throw out your old makeup and buy a new set
32. Empty one junk drawer
33. Take a hobby class
34. Visit a therapist (it certainly helped Robin!)
35. Get a puppy
36. Spray perfume on the sheets
37. Put a nosegay of flowers in every room of the house (even dandelions in a grouping look good!)

Hopefully this list has given you a couple of ideas of things to try. Perhaps it has inspired you to think of some ideas of your own. The key is it has to be something that will give *you* personal pleasure. The activity has to be something you ordinarily would hesitate to treat yourself to. And while you may be limited by time and budget, your "selfish act" should be something that you'll later look back on fondly. The memory should make you smile.

It was two years after Bryan's death before Joan stopped "beating up on herself" as she puts it. She began by pledging to get a pedicure once a month—and forcing herself to keep the appointment. She knew she was making progress when she decided to hire a live-in nanny. With a big smile and utter exuberance she now says, "Sometimes, I even go out!"

While a woman of means might find her selfish pleasure is taking a girlfriend shopping in Paris, another might relish in that silky feeling as she snuggles her feet under the sheets after a relaxing bubble bath.

I personally am "low-maintenance" in this department: my favorites from the list are taking a nap (I still get a cozy feeling when

I think of the snooze I took last January on my sister's couch) and going outside to watch the stars at night. I remember one night I was prepared to lie on a beach towel all by myself, but both Karl and Niki decided to keep me company. The conversation we shared as we speculated about what was out there is one I'll always cherish.

Man does not live by bread alone . . .
. . . but a mom can subsist on crumbs.

Take a moment to think about what you've eaten lately. If you were to write it down and be forced to share the list with someone, would you be embarrassed? Do your four food groups consist of chocolate, strawberry, vanilla, and coffee?

Have you been ignoring your own food needs? Or has your eating pattern become such that the refrigerator's really not safe from you unless it has a padlock?

When Robin's husband walked out, she made sure her children were well fed, as she always has. But she ignored her own diet, stopped eating, and dropped below a hundred pounds.

When I officially left *Today,* I was two months postpartum—but the baby weight was in no danger of disappearing anytime soon. I didn't eat meals—but if a batch of chocolate chip cookie dough might make me feel better, I was willing to try it.

While step number five to getting back on track is to *do something for yourself,* the sub-category is *and that includes eating well*.

The link between food and good health is quite obvious and well reported. The link between food and mood is less well documented, but it *does* exist.

For instance, earlier this century as many as 200,000 people in America suffered from pellagra. One third of those patients died. This was a time when a typical diet consisted of cornbread, fatback, and molasses. In addition to skin and intestinal disorders, pellagra victims suffered depression, psychosis, and in some cases, dementia. In the Southern United States, at one time *half* of the patients in state mental hospitals were demented pellagra victims.

In 1937 all of that changed: the niacin factor was discovered. Pellagra became a thing of the past once people began including foods rich in the B vitamin complex (green leafy vegetables) in their diet.

We've all read recently how important folic acid is for the unborn child. It's important for blood formation and a deficiency in folic acid can lead to anemia.

But studies of psychiatric patients have found them to have levels of folic acid below that of normal persons. And among depressed persons who showed no signs of anemia, 20 percent were found with below normal folic acid levels.

We all remember learning about sailors who contracted scurvy on their long ocean voyages. Once they started sucking limes the disease corrected itself, hence the nickname "limeys." Among the symptoms of vitamin C deficiency are depression, hypochondria, and hysteria.

None of this is to suggest that the problems that have got you rattled will go away if you start to eat your vegetables. But I include this information to drive home the point that nutrition *is* important to overall good health—which includes your mental outlook.

As you may be figuring out, I'm a great believer in lists. I believe in lists because my theory is if you don't have to spend time *thinking about* things, you're more likely to spend the time *doing* what you ought to be doing or would like to be doing.

I also believe the woman in crisis doesn't think well. I want this book and the lists I've spread throughout to do the thinking for you. Are you eating well? No? Well, take a look at the Food Guide Pyramid from the U.S. Department of Agriculture. By consuming the minimum number of servings in each category, you can be assured of getting the right foods you need so you're strong enough to really get back on track.

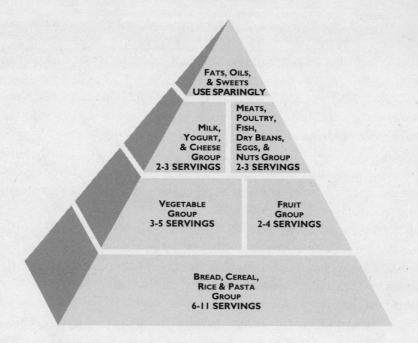

This is not a rigid prescription of what to eat, but a general guide. Stick close to it and you can be assured of a healthy diet.

While we're on the subject of your body, when's the last time you revved your body's engine? How scary is it to see your body in the mirror? Well, let's find out. I'd like you to stand in front of the mirror and see what your body's saying about your level of fitness.

News isn't good, huh? Welcome to the club! Hard as I try, gravity seems to be winning the contest. I worry that soon when I walk, I'm going to be kicking my backside it's starting to droop so low.

Well—there are some miracles even my getting back on track formula can't perform! But you can work a little exercise into even the most busy of schedules to help you feel better about you.

This isn't exercise to lose weight, although if weight is a problem you should work on that once you feel able to fight that battle. This isn't exercise to help you look sexy in a bikini or to catch a man. Any man that is attracted only by a great body, in my opinion, isn't worth wasting one's time on. This exercise is simply to wake up some muscles that have been dormant for a long time. To get the blood flowing to some places it hasn't been in a while.

We're not talking "Jane Fonda feel the burn." This isn't the Denise Austin workout. Stretch. Walk briskly. Take the stairs instead of the elevator. Ideally a good exercise program includes a minimum twenty-minute workout four times a week. That's an admirable goal, but it may be one that is entirely unattainable for you right now.

Just as we began with little baby steps toward the simplest of goals, keep the goals simple and the steps small as you work toward taking care of yourself. Resolve, perhaps, to stretch each morning. Perhaps you can't do twenty minutes of calisthenics, but perhaps you can find time to do twenty sit-ups. Maybe all you've got the time—or inclination—for is twelve leg lifts while holding the back of a chair. Each of these tiny steps, taken over a period of consecutive days and weeks, *will* bear fruit. You will see and feel a difference in your body. More important, you will feel a sense of accomplishment at having chosen a goal and sticking with it.

"Most men pursue pleasure with such breathlessness that they hurry right past it."

—Søren Kierkegaard

The key to step five of getting back on track—do something nice for yourself—is to enjoy the *moment*. Whatever the little pleasure to which you treat yourself, make sure you give yourself the opportunity to enjoy it. While goals are important and having a direction in life is vital, it is equally important to enjoy the moment. As Joseph Campbell put it, "Eden *is*." It is now . . . not the future. We are sometimes so busy improving ourselves and focusing on what is to come that we let the present slip away.

It's like the tourist groups they talk about in Sweden. Years ago my husband was a student helper in a hospital in Stockholm and he was warned to look out for the tourist groups. Seems every year, Swedes would sign up for package tours to places like the Canary Islands. And every year, some of those Swedes would return home only to have a heart attack. They'd worked so hard at having fun they overtaxed their heart. Next time, they'd be well advised to relax a little less strenuously.

How much more fulfilling their vacation would have been had they taken it a bit slower and savored the sun and the sand a bit instead of trying to participate in all the activities that were available.

It's like trying to see Disney World in a day. You probably could hit most of the attractions in one visit. But would anyone in the family enjoy it? The memory of the trip would be one of stressing from attraction to attraction, making sure to hit Space Mountain and Thunder Mountain at strategic times. Splitting up the group so that someone is holding a place in the long lines. What kind of vacation is that?

By the same token, choose one or two pursuits that will give you pleasure. And *enjoy* the sensation of being pampered. Take heart in knowing that you're looking out for number one.

Chapter Seven

BUILDING A NEW YOU

"And ye shall know the truth, and the truth shall make you free."

—John 8:32

To know yourself may truly be the most difficult of all knowledge to attain. "Book learning" as we say in my part of Georgia is something anyone can get, provided you spend enough time in school. While a few subjects may be beyond our grasp, if you had unlimited time to spend in a classroom, you would probably master the material eventually.

But examining oneself can be an uncomfortable and sometimes unpleasant experience. Very few of us haven't made mistakes. I doubt many people reading this book can say they haven't made poor choices. The results of some of those decisions may have had profound impact on our lives—it may have led to the crises we're trying to put behind us now.

Look at Scarlett. How many times did a scene end with her asking, "But Ashley, Ashley, whatever shall I do?"

From her days as a teenager, Scarlett O'Hara had pined away

for the boy from Twelve Oaks Plantation. But all along, he was wrong for her. You and I know that from watching the movie and reading the book. We could see it. But Scarlett never could.

She always thought everything would be perfect if she were with Ashley Wilkes. It wasn't until the end of the movie, when Melanie's dead and Ashley is defeated; when Rhett's walking off into the mist and Scarlett is left alone that she begins to see the man of her dreams—the object of her fantasy—was all wrong for her.

How different might Scarlett's dream have been if only she'd known herself better. Had she known herself better, had she truly opened her eyes to Ashley's weaknesses—she might have made different choices in her life. Some of her crises might not have happened.

"What lies behind us and what lies before us are tiny matters compared to what lies within us."

—Anonymous

The other day I took the car into the shop. That little hole that happened when a pebble bounced up from the highway had now grown into a huge crack that extended all the way across the windshield. As the weather got colder, the crack got bigger. I wasn't thrilled about spending all that money on a new windshield, but I was less excited about driving in November with no windshield at all!

I knew what my problem was—I had a broken windshield.

But when I arrived with the car, the technician didn't look at the windshield at all. Instead, I was interested to see that the first thing the guy at the auto shop did was to check out the rest of the car. He took out a pad with a preprinted picture of a car and slowly, methodically, he walked around the car taking note of any dings or dents to the exterior. *Then* he looked at the crack in the windshield. The cynical reporter in me knew this damage assessment report was to protect the dealer should I claim later that they'd banged up the car.

But it struck me: wouldn't it be smart if we all did a "damage assessment" on our*selves?* If we took a dispassionate view of our lives, our relationships, our feelings, our physical condition?

When you're having a crisis, you *know* what the problem is. Your deadbeat husband walked out, or your job is gone, or your child is ill, or—you fill in the blank. The problem is the *crisis,* right? Well, not exactly. In a crisis, everything feels wounded. We feel betrayed by whomever or whatever we perceived to be the root of our plight. What feels wounded? Do your own damage assessment report.

Have some of your personal relationships suffered?

With whom and how?

Has your physical health changed?

Have you started smoking—or increased the amount you smoke?

Are you gaining weight—or not eating enough to keep the meat on your bones?

When is the last time you exercised?

Do an emotional damage assessment: what could use a little time in the repair shop? Set aside a few pages in your notebook that will be your spot to list your "needed repairs" and "damaged areas."

This won't necessarily be the most enjoyable exercise I'll ask you to undertake. What you are creating is a list of problems—your problems—some of which you may decide to work on.

It wasn't fun at the car shop when the guy told me I needed new brake pads in addition to the windshield repair. On the other hand, I'd rather find out the brakes are worn when the car is safely parked than when I've got to make a sudden stop because a child just dashed in front of me.

It's the same with your damage report. You *know* you are wounded. But when you look closely you may find that there is more than one area that could use care or repair.

We're at the stage of getting back on track in which the reconstruction process is about to get underway. Keep your notebook handy, get out your work gloves, and know that you're about to turn the corner toward a new and better you.

"We must be our own, before we can be others."

—Ralph Waldo Emerson

Do you feel in touch with yourself? Do you have a sense of control about your life? Do the words "placid," "calm," "at peace" in any way describe *you?* Is the way you feel about yourself the way you would want your child or spouse or other special loved one to feel? If not, then you are not "your own."

What Emerson is saying here is before we can fill any of our outside roles—whether they are work-related or simply the interpersonal relationships we have as a friend and family member— we must be comfortable with *who we are.* We have to be comfortable "in our own skin." Accepting of ourselves. Satisfied with who we are.

That's not the same thing as saying we should be complacent and not eager to improve ourselves. Your repair list might be a mile long after your damage assessment. You'll get to those repairs all in good time. First let's get to you.

Time for some changes! The process isn't easy—but I suspect you wouldn't have made it this far in the book if you weren't at least inclined to make some changes in your life. We've done the preliminary work: you've acknowledged that all is *not* right; you've let go of the chores—and the people—who were complicating your life; and you've begun to reinforce yourself by reconnecting with your old friends and by treating yourself nicer.

Now—it's time to put on your hardhat and let's get to it!

• • •

Construction is a lot like childbirth. The process is hell. You go through a lot of wear and tear. But when it's all over, you've got something really incredible to show for it.

Pregnancy is highly overrated. All of us who are moms can recall the moment we first felt the baby kick. We wax poetic about the miracle of giving birth and seeing this living, breathing, screaming little creature emerge from our bodies.

How often have you heard blissful talk about the hemorrhoids and varicose veins? Has anyone ever really enjoyed catching a whiff of an unfamiliar scent and then bolting for the toilet? I've long thought that one of the purposes for all those hormones when you're pregnant is to help you forget all the bad parts.

The process *is* hell. But the final product is worth all the effort. Just like construction.

When we bought our New York City apartment in the late 1980s, it was a disaster. It was a good thing our parents lived so far away. Had they been close enough to New York to see the place, they would have forbidden us to buy it.

The floor was rotted completely away in an area near the kitchen. In one bedroom, it appeared the windows were never closed when it rained. The plaster was disintegrated to the point that the wire mesh and studs showed. To get to one tub, you had to first climb over a toilet.

Fools that we were, we bought the place. We demolished most of it (demolition is cheap, we learned. It's the rebuilding part that will break your budget!). And after months of haggling to get plans approved, trying to imagine just how I'd be using the kitchen, figuring out where electrical outlets would go, and struggling to get the painting done, we moved in.

The painters were wonderful, but I wondered if they'd *ever* leave! One week before Christmas, they were still there and promising to come back after the holidays. I said, "Look, I may work in TV, but my name's not Murphy Brown and you're not Eldin. This has got to end sometime!"

It eventually did—and the final product was an apartment Karl and I were really proud of.

You'll feel the same way after you do your own reconstruction and give birth to a new you!

"Nothing can bring you peace but yourself."

—Ralph Waldo Emerson

When you look in the mirror, what do you see? Physically, how do you appear? Are you sitting down? Then you're not looking in a mirror.

I want you to actually get up, walk into the bathroom or bedroom or get in front of the sliding glass door, and look at your reflection. "No," to answer that little voice that is saying to you, "This is really stupid."

This is *not* stupid. This little trip to the mirror has a point. Stand facing the mirror. Up close. Look at your face. Is there a glow in your eyes, or do they seem lifeless? Lost their shine. Do you have sad, beagle-dog eyes or the eager look of a Yorkshire terrier?

How about your face? Do you look a bit bland and without energy? Does your mouth tend downward into an automatic frown?

Look closely and tell yourself what you see. This isn't a beauty exercise to determine which wrinkle cream you should be considering. Ask yourself, What emotions can you read in your reflection? Could I figure out what's going on in your life, just by looking at your face?

Now step back from the mirror and look at what your body is saying. Is your posture erect? Or do your shoulders curl toward your chest? Is your head resting perpendicularly on your spine? Or does it thrust forward? Where are your hands? Do they naturally tend to rest on the tops of your thighs?

Check out these two drawings: which more closely resembles you?

What is this person on the right trying to tell us? Is it, "Hey, I feel great about myself and you ought to spend some time with me?" Or is the message we're receiving more along the lines of "I hate myself, life is unfair, the world is black—and don't even think about trying to tell me differently."

Which one of these figures best depicts your body message? If you look more like the figure on the right, then your body is saying a lot about your mind-set.

Try this simple trick. Straighten your back and stand with your hands barely brushing the side seams of your pants or skirt. Look what's happened to your shoulders: they've pushed themselves back. They're no longer hunching forward.

This side seams trick was taught to me by Joyce Summey, a woman who nearly twenty years ago helped me prepare for the America's Junior Miss pageant. Joyce had been a judge at my state contest and had worked with several future Miss Americas and their runners-up. Her side seams trick didn't help me win the contest, but it *has* stood me in good stead over the years.

Look at yourself now: hands brushing the side seams, your shoulders are naturally back, your head is resting more correctly on your spine. Be honest: you *look* better now, don't you?

And how do you feel? When you straighten your back, can't you just feel a wave of tension disappear? Hunching your shoulders forward is not easy. It puts a lot of pressure on your upper back. Once you train your body to sit and stand correctly, you'll find that upper back pain to be much less bothersome.

Your own sense of well-being is enhanced as well.

Now look at what you've just done. Very simply, without a lot of exertion and no fanfare, you have done something for yourself that makes you feel better. And this is the you that couldn't do anything right?

Look again at that quote from Emerson: Nothing can bring you peace but yourself. And part of your sense of turmoil may be coming from how you view yourself.

Self-esteem is something we hear talked about ad nauseum. As parents we hope to instill it in our children—as adults, we hope to boost it to conquer new challenges. But what the heck *is* self-esteem?

The best definition I have found came in a newsletter I received at a school parenting group. It described self-esteem as your own concept of you as you *are*—your self-concept—versus your mental image of you as you *ideally should be*—your self-ideal.

In other words, "This is me today." And "This is the way I truly wish that I were." And the distance between those two—the disparity between your self-ideal and your self-concept is your self-esteem. The wider the gulf between what you perceive to be the ideal you and what you believe to be the real you, the greater your lack of self-esteem.

For instance, consider the person who has always been a loner. She didn't join things like the pep club in high school and tends toward sports like golf or tennis, rather than some of the team sports—and to her, this is some sort of flaw. Her picture of the ideal woman is someone with an active social life who is constantly chatting on the phone and dropping by friends' houses. As you might guess, this woman's self-esteem is low because her own perception of the way she is falls short of the way she perceives she ought to be.

STEP NUMBER SIX TO GETTING BACK ON TRACK: BUILD YOUR SELF-ESTEEM

Now we're getting into the reconstruction part of our journey. This is the part that isn't easy. Just as Lamaze exercises prepare a woman to deliver a baby, what we've been working on up to this point will prepare you for this latest childbirth: a newer, stronger you.

When your self-confidence and self-esteem have ebbed to their lowest point, it is virtually impossible to take on something new. So we won't try.

Instead, let's talk about something old and familiar—yourself. And let's work to see if you can't get to know yourself better. Then we'll come back and do a little work with those two images of ourself—the self-ideal and the self-concept.

What is good about you? No. You are not allowed to answer, "Nothing."

When you've been knocked down by crisis, the first thing that goes is your self-image. After all, if you were: smarter/more alert/sexier/thinner/nicer/faster/healthier/more patient and so on, this disaster wouldn't have happened in your life. Well, maybe. And maybe not. We'll do some Monday morning quarterbacking a bit later in Chapter 9.

Are you really as awful a person as you are telling yourself? If you were *that* hideous, don't you think the authorities would have locked you up by now?

Okay, now we're getting somewhere.

You do at least agree with me that you are not a cannibalistic ax murderer.* This is a start. Maybe we can find some other things that are good about you too!

Self-Esteem Exercise No. 1: "What's Good About Me"

Pull your notebook out again and let's make another list. (This notebook is going to become your prized possession.) Start on a fresh page and put at the top of the margin:

What's Good About Me:

Now I want you to list some of your better points. Are you a good cook? Great, then put it down. Are you a loyal friend? Note that. Do you always make time for your children? That's a positive. Do you refrain from swearing? That's a plus in my book. Are you a good reader and retain what you've read? What an advantage! Do you have lovely penmanship?

Explore yourself. Have you any physical attributes that you're proud of? Your hair is naturally a beautiful color? You may be the only woman in America who still has her original shade! I happen to think my nose is rather nice. (Remember I live in New York, which may well be the nose reconstruction capital of the world. A magazine writer for *Vanity Fair* once showed my college documentary to a plastic surgeon to see if I'd had it "worked on"! I wonder what he'd have written if the doctor had said I wasn't "original equipment"?)

Are you organized? Do you keep a nice house? Are your files and papers in order? Have you hobbies that you are good at? Sewing got me through my tough times at NBC. I stitched oodles of curtains and pillows and so forth. You can work out a lot of aggression when you floor that sewing machine accelerator!

---

* If you *are* a cannibalistic ax murderer, could you please go turn yourself in? My suggestions can help in a lot of areas, but I just don't think you can bounce back from cannibalism like you could, say, a crappy divorce.

Are you good at any sports? Maybe you've got the garden that is the envy of the neighborhood. What about your community involvements? Did the Girl Scout cookie sale go well because you handled the business end of things? Perhaps you used to visit shut-ins at the hospital and had an ability to make the older patients smile. What a gift!

Take an inventory of your life and list your accomplishments. Let's go back in time. What awards did you win in high school? What activities invigorated you back then? Are you still doing any of them?

Now, while you've got your thinking cap on and your memory in high gear, I have another exercise for you: has your life always been one of darkness? Be honest—if the answer is yes, then maybe you *do* need to consider getting professional help. Please see the resource pages in the back of the book.

Chances are if you're like most of us, you *can* say the hurt or difficulties or blankness you feel has not been a lifelong event. If you are like most people, the doldrums, depression, blahs, gloominess, or sense of panic you are experiencing now is just an interruption in a life that has been for the most part manageable. Think of a time when life was good for you. Let yourself float back to that period when you were happy. You may want to use some of the relaxation methods from Chapter 4 to help you clear your brain so you can focus on your happy memories.

Rustle up as many pleasant recollections as you can. You may remember big chunks of time which in retrospect seem to have been filled with bliss. Or you may simply recall that warm, fuzzy feeling you had the day you got your first kitten and snuggled your nose in its warm fur. Your memories may be months—they may be moments.

Self-Esteem Exercise No. 2: "My Happy Memories"

Again, pull out your notebook and write down some of these memories. Put it on a page which is headlined: "My Happy Memories."

Recalling some of these happy moments may be difficult. Researchers have found that when you are in a positive (happy) frame of mind, it is much easier to recall positive events. But when you're in a dark mind-set, it is the unhappy time that comes to mind more readily. You may have to struggle to conjure up a happy memory or two, as Robin struggled to find some happy memories that *didn't* include Don. He was a constant presence in her life for the last fifteen years and many of her more recent memories involve him. Even thinking of moments which include her children are bittersweet, as they remind her of the nuclear family that is no more.

There is, however, the glow of being hired for that first job. The excitement she felt when she won a much hoped for promotion. And—as she has now begun to experience the company of other men, she has some new and very delicious recollections.

"Already I've rediscovered what desire is. It's nice to be reminded that someone finds me desirable. It helps your own ego to know someone finds you interesting." The phone call that resulted in a dinner invitation is one of Robin's new happy memories.

Once you have come up with a pleasant past moment, focus intently upon it. Revel in it. Let yourself be filled with the emotions that were part of that time. Are you thinking of the day you won the spelling contest in eighth grade? Bask in the pride of being the best. Recall the congratulations from your teachers and friends. If someone was jealous or unkind when you won, *don't think about it!* We are concentrating only on the good times.

Let the good feelings from that memory help guide you to another happy moment.

Here's a sample from *my* "Happy Memories" page:

- Wearing my lavender cancan skirt my mom made for me when I was eight for a Girl Scout program—I felt so pretty!
- Seeing Karl's bright blue eyes when I finally got to the end of the aisle at our wedding.
- Niki's birth—how the sunlight seemed to fill the room!

- Baking cookies with my mom and sisters and debating which color sprinkles to put where.
- Sitting in Daddy's lap "driving" the car when I was really little.
- Hearing "rumors" that the bosses at NBC liked my work when I "tried out" for the *Sunrise* anchor job.
- The audience response to a series I did on domestic violence—it showed me just how much impact we can have in TV.
- Kyle's beaming face when I enter his room in the morning.

As you can see, my list of happy memories is truly a hodge-podge of events from different times in my life. I still have that lavender cancan skirt. I've stuck it in with all the kids' dress-up stuff. When I see it, I am reminded not only of how pretty I looked wearing it, but also of finding the fabric we made it out of on the remnant table. I recall standing and watching over my mom's shoulder as she sewed the ruffles on her sewing machine. What probably makes me happiest about this memory is that I know this was a time when my mom—who had three other kids, plus a husband, home, and business to worry about—was doing something just for *me!*

That memory is a warm fuzzy. Other memories are moments of pride over achievements. Still others, like my wedding day and the birth of my first son, are moments of almost palpable emotion.

There is no need to analyze *why* these moments make you happy. It is enough to just remind yourself of earlier happy times and have a list of them easily retrievable.

Self-Esteem Exercise No. 3: Build a Positive Self-Concept

Feeling overwhelmed as she often is by the responsibilities that are now hers alone, Caye Allen has more than once felt she's not up to the task. Still, as more time passed since the Oklahoma bombing, she has occasionally allowed herself to feel proud of what she *has* accomplished. And she thinks Ted would be proud of her too.

"We were like Ward and June Cleaver. Our life was dinner and basketball and sports and school plays and carnivals. We did all that stuff." Caye laughs at herself. "Ted and I were so disgusting, we even went to the grocery store together!"

Now it was Caye doing all those things—alone. "When he was alive, I always wanted my husband's approval. I wanted him to think everything I did was good," Caye explains. "And just the other day, I was mowing the yard, making patterns as I went, and I thought, 'Ted would be so proud of the way I've kept this yard up.'

"I know in my heart I'll see him again," Caye continues. "And if there is nothing else that he can say, I want him to be able to say, 'You did a good job. You carried on well. I'm proud of you.'"

The previous self-esteem exercise focused on happy memories. But happiness is *not* just a part of your past. You've simply forgotten how to be happy, because you are overwhelmed by the events that have prompted this turn in your life. What excites you today? No—you are not allowed to say, "Nothing." What brings a smile to your face?

Following are a few fill-in-the-blank sentences that I found as part of some literature to help parents help their children build their self-esteem. I tried it on myself and found them to be *very* useful.

Again, open your notebook (perhaps you shouldn't bother to close it!) and copy down these sentences—adding your own endings:

I am happiest when _____
I am good at _____
I am getting better at _____
People like me because _____
I am lucky because _____

It was this last question that Susie Albert, whose boys are fighting muscular dystrophy, could answer easily. Anyone could pinpoint her bad luck. But equally obvious to Susie was the fact that she has been blessed during her life to have been loved unconditionally.

"Throughout my life," she explains, "I have been lucky in that I have been made to feel that I was special. There was a little something about me that people really loved and thought was kind. And in my marriage, one thing that has gotten me through a lot is that I know that I have been loved."

And why is this so significant? Susie says it goes directly toward self-esteem. "I think if you have been loved, then you know that there is something *to* love. I think that has helped me to handle this a lot. Knowing deep down that I am not alone, that there is something in me that is different than the average person. It has helped me to be strong."

Depending upon the kind of support system you have, you might want to ask some of your close friends or family to complete those sentences with you in mind. Hopefully when you reached out earlier in the book, someone was there to answer your call.

It's not surprising to hear Joan Esposito's self-esteem was pretty well obliterated after Bryan's suicide. Because of her background as a medical reporter, she knew intellectually that *she* was not the cause of his suicide. The "If I'd been a better wife, he might still be here" line was one she stopped repeating to herself within a few weeks.

What Joan couldn't stop was constantly questioning her judgment. "You're walking around going, 'My God! How did I make such a horrible choice? Am I completely stupid? Am I completely blind?' You start questioning *all* decisions you make." And that, Joan says, took a long time to overcome.

When her son, Benjamin, was born nine months later, the self-doubts were especially acute. The natural fears and doubts that any new mother has were amplified to Joan in a way that she *knew* she was a rotten mother.

If she lost her temper—and what mother doesn't? If the baby refused a certain vegetable (my toddler spit an entire mouthful of beans all over me yesterday), Joan read these as confirmation that she wasn't cut out for motherhood. The little bits of progress she would make getting back on track in other aspects of her life were erased by her perceived failures as a mother.

It wasn't until she forced herself to listen to what her friends were telling her that things changed.

"It is only through outside affirmation that it began," Joan recalls. "At first I didn't let it sink in. 'Oh, they're just being nice,' or 'They felt sorry for me.' I mean I was the anchorwoman poster child!" Even in talking about the most difficult period in her life, Joan's wacky sense of humor is never far away.

"Then it started to sink in. I started to go, 'Well, let's just entertain the *possibility* that maybe they're *not* being nice to me and maybe they really do mean it and maybe you're *not* doing this so badly.'" Joan's skepticism at these possibilities at that time is evident, but she figured it was worth at least taking a flyer that someone else's opinion just might be valid.

"I could no longer judge how well I was doing *anything*. But eventually you start to believe. And it took me a long time to realize that, no, actually you are a pretty *good* mother." There is a mix of pride and authority in Joan's voice now. "In fact, you might even qualify as an *exceptional* mother!"

Today on Joan's list of things she's good at, being a mom is top of the list.

Virtually all of Jana Stump's childhood had been centered around athletics. Between her and her sister, Jana was the "boy" of the family. If she couldn't do sports, she reasoned, she couldn't do anything.

Gradually, her eyes were opened to new possibilities. At the rehabilitation hospital, she learned there were sports one could play from a wheelchair. And at school, she gravitated toward activities that previously had been of secondary interest: dramatics and choir. She remembered she was good at singing. When she won the Kansas Junior Miss title, she sang a medley of Disney tunes as her talent presentation.

As Ruth Brody became less dependent upon her daughter for support, she found not only friendship with the women in her cancer support group, but also a need to give back.

"I loved being around these people because they were so happy and so positive and such fighters. They had such an influence on me," Ruth explains, "that I wanted to do the same for someone else."

Ruth took training courses offered by Y-Me and was soon answering calls to the nationwide hotline from her home. It was tough work, and sometimes deeply troubling, as there were frequent reminders to Ruth of just how much she'd gone through herself.

"The memories would come back and it would open some old wounds. There were times I would have to tell them, 'Hey, I need a break for a bit.' But then, women would write the office and tell how much I'd helped them. That was *so* great! It was just wonderful. Hearing that made all the difference!"

Ruth's reservoir of self-esteem was made a little fuller thanks to those callers who took the time to say she'd helped them. Joan's self-esteem grew thanks to the affirmation of many of her friends, whose constant "You're a *great* mom!" finally sank in. But Jana's was a more personal recognition.

If you don't have someone else to complete these sentences about you—or if you're shy or unwilling to ask—it doesn't matter. This is essentially an exercise to help reinforce in your own mind that you do have positive attributes—*and* to give you some specifics about what they are.

By now, your image of yourself should be changing. Go back through the sections of your notebook you've completed. See all the neat things that are on paper about you? There they are—in black and white. Look at all those positive attributes: are these qualities and characteristics one ordinarily associates with someone who is a failure? Of course not!

Now that you are armed with some well-thought-out information about your better points, let's act on them. And let's act on them in a way that gives *you* the chance to get some outside positive reinforcement. Your personal notebook is a great boost, but now it's time for some additional opinions.

Are you a good cook? Great! Then pull out your recipe books, come up with a menu that you *know* you can prepare easily, and invite some friends over for a meal.

It's fine to be honest about why you've suddenly decided to invite guests to dinner. Remember we earlier made a concerted effort to reach out to friends and associates. That wasn't just a one-time project.

"I've been down in the dumps and I thought it might pick me up to have some friends over." That is perfectly honest—and accurate. However, in making your invitation, you can leave out the P.S. to that, which is ". . . and I want you to brag about how good my cooking is so I feel good about myself."

I am a pretty good seamstress. As I mentioned, my dark days were brightened a bit by sewing up a storm. The curtains and bedspreads I made for Niki's room looked terrific, and I was always happy to have a friend over to see the baby—and his nicely decorated room. "I made it myself" was a wonderfully therapeutic thing to be able to say.

In fact, it turns out the act of sewing itself may be therapeutic. A report in the *Journal of the American Medical Association* suggests that women who sew (and there are thirty million of us in America) see a greater drop in heart and perspiration rates and enjoy lower blood pressure. In fact, the destressing and tension-reducing benefits of sewing according to the study are superior even to psychotherapy. I always knew being able to sew was a good thing—but I never expected to hear about *those* kinds of benefits!

So sew yourself silly. Cook up a storm. And bask in the glory. Putting yourself in a position to accept accolades may be difficult. Most women with low self-esteem have a tremendous problem accepting a compliment. There's a sense of "Well, if I'm good at it, it must not be very special or important."

It's not a problem that is limited just to women with low self-esteem. It is, I believe, inherently female. Many women find it very difficult to accept a compliment.

"How nice your hair looks," the typical woman might be told. And she's apt to reply, "Oh! I just came from the salon, it never looks good when I do it." Rather than accept the compliment with a simple thank-you, our typical woman turns what could have been an opportunity to bask in the glow of a kind word into a situation in which she is self-deprecating.

And as hard as it is for most of us to accept a compliment— Wow! Do we find it easy to take to heart every criticism that is ever made about us!

My husband is better than most in offering compliments. When I first started at *Inside Edition,* he would often say "You look really pretty today" when he would get home from work. (What a difference having a professional to help you with your hair and makeup can make! —Oops! There I go, unable to just say, "Thank you.")

If I were to chart out Karl's remarks, I know I would have many more notes in the compliment category than the criticism category. So why is it that what I focus on are his occasionally critical questions, such as, "Well, why *didn't* you mail those bills?"

I get defensive and huffy and indignant and usually launch into a litany of all the things I have to get done during a day. The answer is simply, "I forgot."

I can remember virtually every criticism I've received in the last few years. I wish the compliments stuck as well. As one well-known actress once said, "I remember every bad notice I ever got." Compliments are just hard for women to handle.

While many of us are uncomfortable when we're paid a compliment, we are even more bothered by consciously creating a situation in which the motive is to receive affirmation. "It just ain't fittin'," as Scarlett's mammy would say.

Fittin' or not, that's what I'm asking you to do. Put yourself in a situation or create the situation that you know beforehand will result in some words of praise coming your way. Invite your friends to dinner. Have someone over for lemonade the weekend you know the garden will be at its showiest. Make a flattering dress and take pride in saying, "Oh, I made it myself," when someone asked where it was purchased.

Paint a picture. Write a poem. Put a little bit of *you* into something that you know will be noticed. Try your hair in a new and flattering style. (Come on, don't be afraid, it's only hair. It will grow back if you hate it.) Put yourself in a position to hear something nice about *you*. And then add the warm feeling it gives you to your list of "Happy Memories."

"It is easier to sail many thousand of miles through cold and storm and cannibals in a government ship with five hundred men and boys to assist one, than it is to explore the private sea, the Atlantic and Pacific Oceans of being alone."

—Henry David Thoreau

Who are you? Not what's your name, what do you do, where do you live. But—*who* are you? What do you believe in? What makes you angry/happy? What makes you tick?

Marcia Johnson asked herself that question in the aftermath of her rape. At the time of her rape, she worked as a television news reporter. "He'd told me that he'd been watching me and I couldn't decide if that meant he'd been watching me on TV or if he'd been watching me at the apartment complex." When Marcia did go back to work, she tried to avoid appearing on camera.

"I stopped doing stand-ups. No cutaways. Nothing." Marcia's bosses asked her about it. "They said, 'We've noticed something about your pieces: you're not *there!*' I told them I just could not do it."

Even before her assault, Marcia had already begun to question her profession. She saw the hypocrisy in "warning" the audience against the graphic footage they were about to see, and then running a news report that pushed the envelope in violence and blood.

She took a good look at the work she was doing—and the trends she saw in television news. "I knew that ultimately I couldn't happily make a living at this. I wasn't proud of what I was putting my name on anymore."

Marcia searches for the right words as she tries to explain her thought process. "And, and . . . it had come at such personal cost, that . . . you know. If I was going to live looking over my shoulder [because that guy was still out there], it had to make me proud and make me feel that I was living up to all those notions of journalistic integrity that they painted with their Woodward and Bernstein brushes when I was in journalism school."

Marcia left journalism and got out of television. She now works in the public service field.

Who are *you?* It may be the toughest question you'll ever be asked to answer. I was first asked that question when I was seventeen. Again, Joyce Summey (the lady who helped me get ready for America's Junior Miss) asked me that question. At the time my answer was pretty easy . . . "I'm a seventeen-year-old high school senior who hopes to go to Emory University Law School and become an attorney."

My answer was wrong. Not that I wasn't seventeen or a senior in high school who aspired to a career in law. But that wasn't who I *was.* To say *who I am* at that stage in my life meant to go inward and look at what made me tick. My revised answer then spoke to my new faith as a born-again Christian, my hope that hard work really did pay off with the reward of a goal reached, that I was a fairly serious person who considered herself fairly responsible by virtue of the changes in our home life necessitated by having a mother who was ill.

Mrs. Summey gave me the assignment of taking one page of paper and writing an essay entitled "Who Am I?" She limited me to one piece of paper and prohibited me from using labels to describe myself. I now pass this assignment along to you. I have rewritten my "Who Am I?" essay countless times over the years—sometimes on paper, sometimes mentally. I've always found it time well spent.

Self-Esteem Exercise No. 4: "Who Am I?" Essay

Learn to know yourself. Write a single-page essay entitled "Who Am I?" in which you get to the heart of what you believe is important in life in general and for you in particular. Let this be an opportunity to focus on the life choices you've made and whether they fit the you with which I hope our earlier exercises have helped you reconnect.

This may be one of the hardest tasks I'll give you because there are no right or wrong answers. You are the only "teacher" who will be grading this paper. There is no scoring sheet—you'll just know when you've come up with the description that truly depicts the real you. You'll probably have to take several stabs at this one, and you may not get it right for some time.

Keep trying. And remember, as you get back on track, "who you are" will change. You are growing, becoming stronger. "Who you are" today as you read this will be a very different person, say, a year from now as you continue to grow.

> *One cannot see oneself in running water. Only in still water. Only the still can still the seekers of stillness.*
>
> —Confucius

Remember in Chapter 4, we learned to let go and relax? The distractions you eliminated made it possible to focus on what's important: finding you. This isn't a forever change, although you may find yourself remarkably uninterested in resuming some of the activities you gave up.

Ask yourself: in the course of a lifetime, how much of an absence are you creating by occasionally stepping off the train for just a moment? Use this break to allow yourself the space to discover who you are.

A common denominator in any crisis is the dislocation of one's self-image. Susie's mental picture of her sons playing sports with her husband would never come to pass. Jana could never realistically imagine herself walking. Christina's vision of a houseful of children was shattered. My self-image of a television reporter was gone forever.

When our self-image is taken away, one is left with a huge gaping hole. Without that anchor of self in a crisis, gloom and depression are likely to fill the void.

The closer you can connect to the heart of *who you are*—the fundamentals of your essence as a human being—the less likely you are to be thrown from your foundation when crisis hits. And after a crisis, the more rapidly you can reconnect with your own center, the more quickly you will get back on track.

Have you embraced *society's* label for you? Or will you boldly go forward secure in knowing *who you are?*

Take a moment to reread some of the qualities you've put about yourself in your notebook. You are not what you do, you are not who you've married, you are not the calamities that have come your way. The closer your self-ideal grows to your own self-image, the less important labels will be. The more you value those qualities that you have already identified as traits you possess, the greater your sense of tranquillity.

Look again at those earlier quotes from Emerson: *Nothing can bring you peace but yourself.* And *We must be our own, before we can be others.*

The key to handling life's transitions—whether they be life-altering crises that change the course of our lives forever or the passages we all make from one phase of life to another—depends upon how well grounded we are in our own innate, natural abilities. Stop lamenting what you are *not* and celebrate *who you are!*

Chapter Eight

"THE EXPERTS AREN'T"

"Noah built the Ark, the experts built the Titanic. *"*

A FEW THOUSAND YEARS BACK, Noah was just an ordinary farmer trying to live right and take care of his family when God called him. God said, "Hey, Noah. There's going to be some rough weather coming your way—forty days and nights of rain! You'd better drop what you're doing and build an ark."

Now Noah was a good man and more than anything he wanted to please God. But Noah felt obliged to remind God that he knew nothing about ark building.

"No problem," God said. God told Noah to stick with Him, just follow His directions and he'd do just fine.

And indeed, Noah's boat was just perfect to hold one pair of all the animals plus the food plus Noah's family. We all know what happened next. Rains came, boat worked great, water finally receded, and the story had a happy ending.

Noah was an amateur. Had no ark-building experience whatsoever.

Now ask yourself: who built the *Titanic?* Yup, the experts.

(For those of you a bit rusty on your history, the supposedly unsinkable luxury liner sank in 1912 after hitting an iceberg on its maiden voyage.)

Like I said, "The experts aren't."

Have you noticed lately how dependent we've become on "experts" as a society?' You can't watch a news show or read a magazine without being bombarded by them. Think back to the O.J. Simpson trial—if you had a law degree and could put four words together, you could become an "expert commentator" on television about the case. And yet, when the jury announced just four hours into deliberations that they were ready with a verdict, how many of the experts guessed it right?

Yes, I've included some expert studies and findings in this book. They are included for those of us who are still expert-dependent. They serve to bolster what is really a commonsense approach to taking charge of your life. I'm just an amateur who has come up with some ways to put life's doldrums behind you. A lot of what I'm sharing isn't particularly scholarly. But for some of us, the commonsense statement seems more believable if we hear that an expert has come to the same conclusion.

In many ways, experts have become a crutch, an excuse for the wrong moves we make in life.

Seek out the experts' advice and do what they suggest. If it goes wrong, well, "I was only following what the experts said . . ."

My business is overrun with experts. We've got consultants who evaluate our shows, experts who'll tell you a wood floor is more friendly than a tile floor, focus groups interpreted by experts to tell you what the public thinks—and consultants who know *everything*. Some of them have actually even *worked* in television!

Relying on experts somehow absolves us of the responsibility of our mistakes in life. We needn't feel bad about ourselves, because it wasn't really we who made the mistake. It is simply that the experts were wrong.

And yet we still keep leaning on the experts.

STEP SEVEN TO GETTING BACK ON TRACK: TRUST YOUR GUT

The hardest thing in the world to do when you are in the throes of a crisis is to trust your gut. After all, if you were so smart, would you be in the fix you're in right now?

It's very easy to second-guess yourself when you're wounded. Perhaps your crisis is a health problem. "Who knows?" you tell yourself. "If I'd taken better care of myself/eaten my vegetables/reduced my fat intake/visited the doctor maybe this wouldn't be happening."

If the trouble is professional, you might ask, "Was I too accommodating/too bossy/not at my desk enough" to merit that promotion?"

It's what I call the "woulda, coulda, shoulda" life. "If only I'd . . . " You fill in the blank.

"Obviously," you tell yourself, "if only I were smarter this wouldn't have happened." So for me to tell you to rely upon your instincts seems like totally useless advice. "That might work for some people, Deborah," you may be saying. "But I'm the one who's in this mess."

Yes—and you can get yourself out of it too.

> *"Doubt is precisely what makes a culture grow."*
>
> —Tristan Vox

It's a natural outgrowth of a crisis. When the unexpected happens, who wouldn't find their faith in themselves shaken? Stuff like this doesn't happen to smart people, right?

Stuff like this is what makes people smart. And the doubts you may have about yourself and your ability to make smart choices will be the key to the *new stronger you* you are working toward.

Doubt *is* what makes one grow. Whether you are a nation or a nitwit.

Think about it. How would history have read if a group of colonists hadn't had serious doubts about the way King George III was administering this place called the American Colonies?

The question of the propriety of American men fighting in Vietnam led to an antiwar effort that eventually resulted in the U.S. withdrawal.

Today most of us no longer work under the illusion that the employer we have today will be our employer for life. And the doubt that any one job will be ours forever prompts us to keep current on technology and stay sharp on our skills.

Do you really believe Social Security will be there to take care of you in your old age? (Remember, those people in Washington are *experts!*) I don't. And the doubt that my Social Security contributions are being well managed prompts me to study harder and try to make wise investment decisions.

I want the best education possible for my boys. And my concern (read: doubt) about the public schools in my area forces me to look closely at all the educational options that exist.

There! Five good things—three current, two historical—to come from doubt.

Need more? Let's go back further in history. Remember the story of David and Goliath? The Israelites were quaking in their boots over the Philistines, particularly that gargantuan they called Goliath. And they'd gotten into this ridiculous situation in which there would be a winner-take-all duel. The side which lost would become the slave of the victor.

None of the Israelites would take on Goliath. He was, as we say in the modern vernacular, "one mean mother."

But David, a young boy, who was only at the battle site because his father asked him to bring food to his older brothers, spoke up.

"I will fight the Philistine," he said.

Well, his brothers were furious a) that he was there, and b) that he was proposing something so stupid as to fight this maniacal enemy. Any expert could have told you the boy was doomed in taking on Goliath. But David's gut told him otherwise. After all, he'd protected himself in the past against lions and wolves. "How different was this?" he wondered.

King Saul was impressed by the boy and his thoughtful questions. He gave him permission to take on the opponent.

You know the story: David refused the King's sword and shield, preferring to fight with his homemade slingshot. And of course, he flung a rock at Goliath, killed him outright, and was rewarded for his victory.

The story of David is the story of an *amateur* with a *belief in himself* (and his God) going forward in the face of doubt. He trusted his gut—and it didn't serve him wrong.

Doubt is precisely what makes a culture grow.

Doubt is precisely what padded Joan Esposito's bank account and provided financial security for her baby boy too. The ugly rumors that had been passing through Chicago and finally articulated on the radio circulated for a couple of months before the impact of what was being said finally hit Joan. It was April or May—about three months after Bryan's death.

The *National Enquirer* had finally gotten wind of the gossip and the story of an anchorwoman's husband driven to suicide because she was carrying a professional athlete's baby was just too juicy to pass up. Everyone *knew* it was true, right? After all, as the old saying goes, "If you don't sue, it must be true."

When Joan heard of the pending *Enquirer* piece, she hired the toughest legal guns she could find: Dan Webb, a former U.S. Attorney in Chicago, and Howard Pearl, a respected litigator. They took affidavits from the "rumored father" of Joan's baby who stated that he not only did not know Joan, but had never even met her. As Joan explains it, the lawyers wanted to show the *Enquirer* the lawsuit they would file if they went ahead with their story. It would mean an automatic victory in court for Joan if the story ran.

The *Enquirer* killed the piece.

But that didn't kill the rumors. It was several months later that

Joan realized as she became more visibly pregnant, the rumors circulated more rampantly. Joan asked her friends and her lawyers what she should do.

I remember advising her to sue. I said to Joan, "If you sue, you *will* win. It's the only legacy Bryan can give your baby."

But the experts had other opinions.

"Both Dan and Howard met with me separately to try to talk me out of going to court," she says. "Dan told me if it ever gets to trial it will be like a rape trial in that the victim will be the one on trial. He said, 'Just turn the other cheek.'"

Joan relates the conversation crisply and matter-of-factly. "'No,' I said. 'You're wrong. I've been quiet too long. The fact that I've *been* quiet lent credence to the rumors.'"

Joan told the lawyers to sue. They still tried to talk her out of it. "They said, 'Your whole past history will be on trial!'" Joan laughs. "I said, 'Tell me something the public *doesn't* know about me? They know who I've married, who I've divorced, who I've lived with . . . ! It's all already out there!'"

And on Tuesday, September 21, 1993, seven and a half months after Bryan's death, Joan Esposito filed an $8 million defamation lawsuit against WBBM-FM radio and its morning disc jockey, Joe Bohannon.

The lawsuit included the offending comments. March 24: "There is a newswoman in Chicago who we all know and love who is carrying one of the Bulls babies. . . . You just sit there and scratch and you think about that: Which Chicago Bulls baby is right now in the uterus of what Chicago newswoman?"

The lawsuit was a huge news story in Chicago and had immediate impact. Because Joan had gone to court, people were forced to take notice. Grudgingly many people acknowledged they *had* believed the rumors—even though there had been no basis in fact for them. As one local columnist put it, "Going public [with the lawsuit] was a courageous and defiant act." He closed his essay by saying the public owed Joan "an apology. In advance, here's mine."

Joan followed her gut—*not* the advice of the experts. Nine months after filing suit, she reached a settlement with the radio station for an undisclosed sum and a public apology. While Joan cannot discuss the details of the settlement, one Chicago paper reported the amount in excess of $1 million.

The experts aren't.

I admire Joan and her courage so much—more than I have ever told her. I know how difficult it was for her to summon up the bravery to go to court. I wish I could have been as strong of heart during my purgatory by the press.

Not following my gut is my one regret from the whole *Today* show mess.

For weeks, the media unloaded its artillery at me. I shared some of what they had to say earlier. After what seemed like the five hundredth ugly article, I went to the press bosses and said, "Please let me talk to these people! We've got to address these remarks."

But NBC chose the ostrich method of dealing with negative press. They felt it best to do and say nothing. In fact, they ordered me to say nothing as well, putting a gag order on me. It was my understanding that keeping my job was connected to my staying quiet.

"Trust us," the head lady told me. "We're experts at this." Well, based on the way everything turned out, I now have some pretty strong opinions about experts in general. The experts aren't. If I ever get enough time to do a needlepoint pillow, that's what it will say: "The Experts Aren't!"

First thing we do, let's kill the experts.
(With apologies to William Shakespeare)

Linda and Gary Thomas learned all about experts when their daughter, Marisa, was born. It was their first child and Linda's pregnancy had been happily uneventful. During the week, she went about her job as an advertising executive and Gary was busy with his work as a mechanical engineer. On weekends they worked on getting their house in order, building a new bedroom for their expected bundle of joy.

When Marisa arrived, they could barely describe their happiness. She was a beautiful little girl and perfect in every way. At least that's what the doctors told them. Then just minutes before the Thomas family was about to leave the hospital and take Marisa home for the very first time, a neonatologist came to Linda's room.

"I don't know how to tell you this," he started. His face was somber. His voice had a touch of sadness to it. "There is something terribly wrong with Marisa."

Linda and Gary couldn't believe it. Their little girl was perfect. Her APGAR scores were excellent and, to their families at least, Marisa was clearly the most beautiful child in the nursery.

The doctor went on to explain that Marisa had been born microcephalic, an extremely rare condition which meant her brain was small and would never grow to normal size.

Linda recalled that dark day. "He said, 'She'll never walk, she'll never talk. She'll be blind. She won't be able to dress herself or feed herself or do anything.'" And the doctor's final prediction was the worst: "She probably won't even know you're her parents."

"It was devastating," Gary remembers. "We'd gone from being on top of the world to having our world fall to pieces."

The Thomases' next weeks became a maddening blur of visits to medical specialists to learn more about possible treatments or therapy. They inquired what became of other children who had the same kind of problem. One visiting nurse held out precious little hope. "You'd be better off just putting her in an institution and trying again," was the reply.

For Linda and Gary, the doctor's devastating prognosis was the crisis they could have never imagined or prepared for. Their much wanted, much anticipated baby was profoundly handicapped. And the expert advice was "Give up on your little girl—there is nothing that can be done."

That advice wasn't something the Thomases could accept. Their gut told them there *was* help to be found, that somehow Marisa could enjoy more than the vegetative existence the doctor was outlining for them.

If faith alone were all it took, Marisa would be a normal, active little girl. Time after time, her parents would seek out specialists who might be able to work with Marisa and help her overcome her handicaps. Repeatedly they were let down. Linda put hundreds of miles on the car, driving to specialists for consultation—only to be given another grim prognosis.

When doctors found Marisa was beginning to collect fluid around the brain, Linda was sent to yet another specialist at Mount Sinai Hospital in New York City for a consultation. "I showed him the CAT scans," Linda remembers, "to see if Marisa was a candidate for a shunt. And Dr. Aaron said, 'These CATs are really bad. This is as grave a situation as I have ever seen. But,' he went on to say, 'I have seen children with CATs as bad as these and they've gone on to do things you wouldn't believe.'"

It was a turning point for the Thomases. "He gave us the first glimmer of hope from a medical professional," Linda states emphatically. "And I said, 'Let's go for it!'"

The operation was a success and once again, as her parents already felt she had, Marisa had proved the experts wrong. She definitely knew who her mother and father were. Like any other child, her behavior was dramatically different when mom and dad were around than when her grandparents or another caregiver was present.

Marisa *did* know what was going on! Linda was quite sure. Marisa had her own way of saying hello in the morning. An uttering that later took the form of "Hi-ya!"

"Hi-ya" was a combination "Hello, I am fine and I'm glad you came here to get me" greeting to her parents.

A day that started with Barbra Streisand was always going to be a good day. Gary would put on a Streisand cassette and spend the first few minutes of the day dancing with Marisa in her bedroom. That look of unbridled happiness on Marisa's face was a clear contradiction of the experts who said this little girl would never know joy.

The years went by. Linda and Gary never wavered in their

search for the key to unlock the little girl they knew Marisa to be. Her daily dance with Streisand became augmented by other favorite bits of music. And when Linda and Gary needed to see a smile on Marisa's face, they could always count on musical toys and electronic pianos.

Gradually, it began to dawn on them: music had an importance to Marisa unlike anything else. Instinctively, Linda knew the key to reaching Marisa would be found in music. Energized by this realization, powered by the intuitive knowledge that only a mother can have, Linda resumed her search for Marisa's salvation. She knew that someday, somewhere she would find the music program that would help her little girl reach her greatest potential.

It was a private search. After sharing her thoughts with Gary, who was convinced Linda was on the right track, Linda spread her net again, hoping to find a therapy program that utilized music.

For the longest time, it seemed maybe the doctors were right. Linda kept running into one dead end after another. Then she heard about a clinic in New York City. It was about an hour and a half's drive from their New Jersey home, but what she'd heard sounded promising: the Nordoff-Robbins Music Therapy Clinic used music to reach physically and mentally challenged children who were unresponsive to other programs.

It sounded like the answer to their prayers.

"We don't promise to cure children," clinic founder and director Clive Robbins says. "But we do work to help every child reach her fullest potential."

Those first sessions were horrific. For the full twenty-five minutes, Marisa initially did nothing but scream.

Eventually, Marisa stopped screaming, her natural curiosity drawing her closer to her therapists. Gradually, music helped the little girl feel a sense of control in the world she could not see. In her music sessions, if Marisa tapped a tambourine, her therapist struck a piano chord. If Marisa sat there, nothing happened. For the first time ever, *she* could orchestrate the actions of an adult.

To help build strength in her weak little legs, Marisa was

taught to jump from one large drum to another, always in time with the music.

The joy and confidence from the lessons spilled over to home life. Two years after beginning music therapy, Marisa was able to hold a cup and drink by herself. Four years after beginning therapy, Marisa was feeding herself and beginning to talk. She was graduated from Nordoff-Robbins and now enjoys horseback riding therapy and second grade, where she is a student in the multiple-handicaps program.

The little girl who would "never walk, or talk, or know her parents," still doesn't walk, but she has exceeded all the *experts'* expectations. Her parents always knew she would!

"Each man is his own star."

—Ralph Waldo Emerson

One of my favorite memories as a child is watching *The Wizard of Oz* with my sisters. It came on television every year, usually around Halloween. It was a special time for us: we'd all curl up on the floor of the den, huddled around a huge bowl of buttered popcorn. (We didn't get popcorn very often, as I recall. Maybe that's why I liked *The Wizard of Oz* so much.)

We all had our favorite parts. I was bored to tears during the black-and-white part when Dorothy was in Kansas. When those creepy monkeys made an appearance or those nasty trees started throwing apples, all four of us would dive under Mom's handmade afghan.

As I grew older, I became more aware of the allegory behind the search for the Wizard. I grew increasingly annoyed with the Lion and the Scarecrow and the Tin Man for going through such hell when they didn't really have to. They already had the courage and the brains and the heart they sought, but didn't know it.

Even *they* required an expert—the Wizard—to validate them. When they viewed themselves from a different vantage point, they recognized their traits. As we all know, courage, intelligence, and caring are not tangibles which can be held. The Wizard gave the adventurers a heart and a diploma and a testimonial, but of course they were meaningless trinkets.

However, when the Wizard presented the gifts it changed the characters' *views of themselves*. They now had a belief in themselves. Faith that they possessed courage, intelligence, a heart. It was there all along—their newfound faith and self-confidence helped them recognize it.

"Follow the Yellow Brick Road. Follow the Yellow Brick Road."

—Munchkins to Dorothy, in *The Wizard of Oz,* by L. Frank Baum

How do we get to that Emerald City of confidence that will allow us to trust our gut and realize that the experts aren't? The good news is, your journey needn't be nearly as frightening as Dorothy's was. And the bad news? Well, the trail is not half as well marked!

They say women are born with a heightened intuitive ability. That may be true, particularly when it comes to knowing something's wrong with their children. But most of us are not psychic. When it comes to intuition, like the Lion and his courage, we aren't looking in the right place to find it.

Can you develop your intuition and make your gut more trustworthy?

Definitely! It's a process of trial and error—with the emphasis on *error*. Only through making some mistakes will you learn the soundness of your instincts. But just as a baby doesn't really learn the meaning of the word "hot" until he gets burned, you may have to get stung a bit to fully develop your own powers of intuition.

"As soon as you trust yourself, you will know how to live."

—Goethe

Developing your intuition, learning to trust your hunches, and following your inclinations is the process that involves focusing on your own life experiences and exploring the different ways they might have played out.

The next time you have a decision to make or problem to resolve, try to see if you can't hear what your inner voice is telling you to do. Don't sit there and say you don't *have* an inner voice— we *all* do! Have you ever started a sentence and then heard in your mind, "Oh Lord, don't say that!" as you proceed to make a fool of yourself? That was your inner voice speaking.

Emerson said, "Your inner voice is best heard in the quiet of solitude."

Find somewhere where you can be alone, where the phone won't be ringing, where for a few minutes at least no one can bother you. Focus on the decision to be made. Do you have an initial hunch about what's the best step to take? What are the facts that you know about the situation? Think about the various solutions or actions that you *could* take with respect to this issue. Mentally, follow each possibility out to its conclusion. There may be forks along the various paths—take each and see where they lead you.

I'd recommend you go through the process with your eyes closed, visually traveling each possibility. I do my best thinking lying down—which is why it always takes me so long to fall asleep at night. At night, when the rest of the world is asleep, I'm busy solving the world's—and my—problems! Perhaps you prefer to take a pad and paper and graph out your options.

Start with a relatively simple issue, such as "Should I take that weekend getaway?" This is an exercise to help you *develop* your intuition. "Should I stay in this marriage or not" is not the kind of question I want you to be focusing on right now!

What follows is an example of a dilemma and the various possible solutions:

PROBLEM: _____

YES: NO:

_____   _____

_____   _____

_____   _____

THEN . . .   THEN . . .

_____   _____

_____   _____

_____   _____

Now go back and ask yourself: was your first hunch on the money?

Try this process every time you have an issue to deal with. You should find problem solving becomes easier because you learn to trust your instincts. Don't skip the exercise. Just as good penmanship or becoming adept at a sport takes time, learning to trust your gut is an endeavor.

It's also time well invested. How much easier it will be to resolve the next big problem you face, knowing your inner compass is properly calibrated and will lead you where you ought to go.

This process should also open your eyes to another important fact: there is no *one* right answer. As a child, my eyes were first opened to the world beyond my tiny Georgia hometown thanks to the *National Geographic*. My parents had decades of the distinctive yellow-bound magazine filling the shelves of our bookcases.

Countless school reports by the Norville kids were jazzed up courtesy of the *Geographic* and its variety of story topics.

The average story in *National Geographic* takes about *four hundred rolls of film!* Of the fifty photographs that actually end up in the article, over fourteen thousand were considered. Obviously, there were not 13,950 *bad* photographs—but simply fifty that stood out above the rest when the photo decisions were being made.

Photographer Dewitt Jones has talked about what makes a photograph extraordinary enough to make the final selection. In a word, risk. He says, "Time and again, I've found that it's the ability to risk possible failure that has led me from a good shot to an extraordinary shot."

Jones says the key to a great picture is finding the right lens. If his initial perspective is not correct, he says he knows he doesn't have a chance of finding a great solution to his photographic problem. By changing perspective, in a photographer's case, switching lenses around, a different solution might present itself.

Creative thinking, tapping in to one's intuition is much the same. Viewing the problem from many perspectives, from different angles also highlights the fact that *more than one solution* can be correct. It is easier to trust your gut, when you know there is more than one right answer.

With their new perspectives courtesy the Wizard, Dorothy and the others saw the solutions to their problems. They learned, as you will, "to trust themselves," as Goethe put it, thus "knowing how to live" and how to make *good* decisions.

Your decisions will be good only to the extent that they are *right* for you.

By now, you've done the roadwork necessary to make those right decisions. Reread some of the pages you've put in your notebook.

- You have talents and skills that make you feel good about yourself.

- You have a bank of happy memories to take you to a time when you didn't feel paralyzed by crisis.
- You've been taking care of yourself and being nice to *you*.
- You've got a clear sense of who you are and what makes you tick.
- You've worked to perfect your problem solving and sharpened your intuition.
- You no longer need the experts to guide you. You've set your own compass and can find your way. Trust your gut—it won't let you down.

Chapter Nine

WHAT HIT ME?

"The unexamined life is not worth living."

—Plato

WE'VE ALL HEARD IT BEFORE: experience is the best teacher. But just what exactly is it we're supposed to be learning?

The aftermath of a crisis is very much like the first moments after a car crash. You check for broken bones and after determining that the injuries are not life-threatening, you may ask: what hit me?

HARD AS IT IS, STEP EIGHT TO GETTING BACK ON TRACK: ANALYZE WHAT HAPPENED

You may or may not be able to make sense of your crisis. You may or may not be able to find the cause of it. Perhaps you'll find where you made some wrong choices and helped create the current difficulties you're confronting. Perhaps not. At the very least, we are going to try to understand *what* happened. The whys we'll tackle later.

You've experienced a loss. You may feel as though you are a failure. Maybe you *are* a failure. But that is not a judicial sentence you will wear forever like Hester Prynne's scarlet letter. You *can* and *will* succeed again.

Robin knew that the moment Don told her he just wasn't happy in the marriage. "I always knew I would survive . . . from the first moment Don did this to me. I knew I would survive." Robin's words are hopeful, but her voice is thin with weariness. She is still waiting for some emotional confirmation of what she intellectually knows to be true. Her counseling is helping.

"Last fall, after several months of therapy, I knew that I would survive it well. I now know there will be a future. There might even be a fabulous future, I don't know." Robin is still trying to get back on track from her breakup. She's hoping that time and talking about her feelings will help her feel better about the loss she still doesn't quite understand.

From our earliest moments on earth until our last breath, our existence is focused in large part on acquiring. We collect things, we gather friends, we amass savings, we build achievements. The emphasis is on *more* and *better.*

A crisis highlights what we have *lost:* a job, a spouse, one's health, public stature. The loss of these things is an embarrassment. Tangible proof that we have failed. The focus is on what's missing. The emphasis on what has slipped away.

But what *if* that isn't what this life-changing situation is *really* all about? What if there is something to be learned from what's happened? You can mourn your loss—*and,* you can learn from it.

"Those who cannot remember the past are condemned to repeat it."

—George Santayana

We've all seen that quote since our first history teacher used it to justify those hours focusing on events that happened centuries ago. The study of history *is* important. The focus on your own history can yield a lot more useful information than Miss Claridge's seventh-grade class.

In looking back on her two-year ordeal with breast cancer and all the related surgeries, Ruth Brody has some very firm opinions. "I would certainly handle things differently today because I am so much smarter. I got five different opinions, but they were all from the same facility. I should have gone to another facility because there is a different school of thought. I believe I might have had a lumpectomy and conserved the breast."

Had Ruth chosen that course of treatment, she might have avoided the three additional surgeries she had because of complications with her breast implant.

When I look at what happened to my career, I still find it a bit amazing. The switch from Golden Girl to goat was astonishingly quick. And while I know what *happened*—who said what, which article appeared where—to this day I still have a hard time trying to figure out what, if anything, I could have *done* to stop it. The NBC News freight train seemed to be out of control.

Yet, when I look at that difficult chapter in my life, when I go back over some of the other periods that have been trying, I see a common thread to all the rough spots in my life: I should have followed my instincts. During that horrible period at *Today,* the only thing I now wish I'd done differently was speak up.

Yes, I know the experts had said I should let them handle the press. But my heart was telling me to respond to those press attacks. Instinct said, "Defend yourself." Intuition said, "You know better how to deal with this than they do." I don't think that was grandiose thinking on my part.

Recently I spoke to a class of journalism students in Florida at the University of Miami. Their professor was one of my old bosses at NBC—one of the guys who helped decide to hire me, in fact—Joe Angotti. When a student asked me about the *Today* debacle, Joe spoke up and said, "Deborah was the only one who was trying to put the brakes on her going to *Today*. She was the only one saying 'go slow.'"

Funny, I didn't know anyone had heard me then!

Again, I should have followed my instincts. And just as in the previous chapter some of the exercises were directed toward helping you trust your own compass, the hindsight of time has helped reaffirm to me that my instincts back then were probably correct.

I know now, I screwed up. I should have listened and acted on my intuition.

For Joan, looking back at the tragedy of Bryan's death and all the troubles she endured afterward, the lessons learned were different. With the distance of some time, Joan was able to understand that she couldn't have helped a condition she didn't know existed. She didn't know about Bryan's earlier suicidal comments and action. She couldn't fight a demon she didn't realize was lurking nearby.

Susie knows that she could not have prevented the tragedy of her sons' disease. That type of genetic screening was not routinely available when she was pregnant with her sons. But what she has learned since Jack's and Sam's diagnosis has helped her get in touch with geneticists who will be able to determine if her daughters might also carry the damaged gene. Susie may have a lot of questions, but not on this subject. "I do think it was important to get to the bottom of this and bring an end to this disease. Testing my daughters is one way to prevent them from going through this kind of tragic situation. That is one way that I can protect them."

When Robin went back through the recent years of her marriage, she realized that Don had been emotionally absent for a long time. She recognized that as much as four years had passed since there had been any real joy in her marriage.

And she is starting to grasp what may have happened that led her marriage to this disastrous end. "I think it all boils down to unresolved issues. Maybe a marriage lasts forever because those unresolved issues mesh so well. But if the equation changes—it could be children, sometimes a career changes it, sometimes other people come along—then those things that helped you be supportive of one another start to tear you apart.

"Don had a lot of problems with his mother. And when I became a mother, he expected me to fail—because *she* did. His mother would often get sick and Don would have to care for her." And Robin sees some unfinished business from her childhood that impacted on the way she reacted as a married woman. "When my dad was on a rampage, beating my brother and sister, if I got sick, he would stop and not hurt them." Robin saw working herself into exhaustion and sickness as a way of bringing the family together. For Don, such illnesses were a reminder of the mother he did not admire.

"If I had to do it all over again, I'd make the same mistakes, only sooner."

—Tallulah Bankhead

Woody Allen was wrong when he said 99 percent of success is showing up. Success is *not* just showing up. It's making mistakes and learning from them. Robin doesn't know if there will be another relationship in her life. She's still trying to get over the trauma of this one ending. But if there is, Robin will go into it very differently.

Cynthia doesn't spend a lot of time looking back at their foray into the car business and the market crash that cost them everything. For months there was no time for reflection. Cynthia was busy working two jobs trying to earn enough money to keep from losing the house. She scrambled to keep the mortgage current while David sought a new career. He got a job as a social worker in their hometown. And after a year and a half of pinching pennies and praying, the Greens sold their house.

When pressed today to do so, Cynthia looks back on that period as one during which God was at work. "We were becoming so materialistic," she says. "Anything we wanted, we were going to get. We were forgetting to make a regular contribution to church work.

We were not as active in the church as we needed to be. We basically dropped most of our friends. We were just working all the time.

"I think what happened was a kind of wake-up call. It was like God saying, 'You don't need all this stuff, you need Me.'" Cynthia is reflective. "He was saying, 'You need to get back to the gifts I have given you of working with people and this is not it.' Now, I can say that."

"How long before you came to this realization?" I asked Cynthia.

"Several years," she said. "Several years."

We don't watch a lot of television in our home, but one show I do encourage Niki to see is on PBS on Sundays, *Magic School Bus*. It's a wonderful animated series which teaches kids about science through the adventures of a class driven around in a magical bus by a wacky woman named Miss Frizzle.

Miss Frizzle's motto is: "Get messy, make mistakes."

It's the opposite of what most of us are usually told as kids. Most of the time as children we were admonished to stay clean. Too often grown-ups intervened to help us do something. That usually meant do it for us.

But the lucky ones among us had a Miss Frizzle in our lives. We were allowed to make mistakes. We were encouraged to take risks. We were cheered for taking chances. If we got messy, that was a part of the learning process. Only by doing it wrong did we learn to do it right.

That's the point in *looking back*. To gain a greater understanding of how the actions we took—and the actions of others—resulted in the frustrations, setbacks, sense of failure we are trying to now combat.

Have you been living what Joseph Campbell would call a myth? In his book *The Power of Myth,* Campbell talks about the role myth has traditionally held in human society. Myths were the first stories, the explanations man created for those things he could not understand: the rise and set of the sun, the change of the seasons, the natural cadence of life. They were grounded in the realities of the world around us, but there was a fancifulness, a bit of fiction to these myths.

In more modern times, the philosopher Carl Jung asked, "What myth are we living?" Is your life being dictated by a myth that is based upon reality—you are a mother, a wife, an office-worker—that forces you to live a fiction that is not *right* for you?

In the neighborhood where we live, most of the mothers are stay-at-home moms. I often feel I am one of the few moms making the suburbs-to-city commute—and a big part of me longs for the morning tennis games, the spots on the school fund-raiser commit-tees, and the leisurely cups of coffee that I know my girlfriends can often fit into their schedules. But that myth would not be right for me and I am in tune with myself enough to know it. If I didn't get the stimulation of delving into the day's events, of watching stories break over the wire services, the rush of delivering my television scripts, I would long for it—no matter how much I adore my boys and my husband.

Instead, I have created my own reality which may not bear much resemblance to my friends' lives, but it is right for me and my family. I am home with my family virtually every night—not on an airplane. I get the interaction with the other moms on an occasional basis and during *Inside Edition*'s summer breaks—which helps me feel charged as a mother and a part of our community. I created the myth that is right for me by consciously rejecting the myths that so-ciety or my community might have dictated for me.

Examine the myths that have guided you in the past. When you look back at the screenplay that has been your life, what role are you playing? Are you constantly starring as the victim? Do you see events as happening *to* you as opposed to being controlled *by* you? Are you constantly acquiescing, always giving in? Do you fre-quently subjugate your desires and wishes to accommodate some-one else's? Are you reinforcing what psychologists have called "learned helplessness"?

"One of the big things I lost was my sense of being safe."

Among the side effects of Bryan's suicide was that Joan, formerly an assertive, independent, self-reliant sort, had become fearful. She couldn't put the image of his body out of her mind, and the security that she lost with his death made everything else seem less secure too.

"You're in a fairly normal relationship and suddenly everything is 180 degrees," she explains. "I have lost my sense of being safe. I went out and bought the safest, biggest, tanklike car that I could find. My whole life since this thing happened is geared toward being safe. And I have yet to regain that."

Joan is well on her way toward combating that fear. "A friend told me that people live their lives according to their fears or their dreams. The one thing Bryan's life has done is make me decide to live life according to my dream."

Is being a victim your dream? Then *stop*. In the last few years, it has been fashionable to blame one's current misfortunes on one's past victimhood. Nowhere has that been more visible then in our legal system. The Menendez brothers killed their parents because they had been victimized as children. Abuse is a terrible thing and should be punished. But the jury ultimately decided the victims should not attempt to redress the abuse by committing first-degree murder.

In my own story, eventually the label affixed to me changed from schemer to victim. And while the victim label seems to more accurately peg the role I had in the melodrama, it was never one I particularly cared for.

To me, being called a victim was a pejorative, an insult. It insinuates that one is powerless to control his own destiny. Maybe for a time one *is* unable to control the events that have sent your life spinning, but I see it as a temporary condition.

The victim label is a more palatable way of saying "failure." Which would you rather be called? Of course. A victim is a figure that evokes sympathy. Kind thoughts are directed their way.

A failure is a loser. A failure is an outcast. A situational leper. No one wants to get close, lest the cloud of disaster rain on them too!

Forget about thinking of yourself as a victim. And don't you *dare* call yourself a failure.

Maybe you *don't* have control over the events in your life right now. But you can change the way you look at the events.

No one can make you a victim if you don't let them.

Giving up victimhood—saying goodbye to "poor little me"—is exhilarating. Letting "stuff happen" is liberating. And freedom can be scary.

As Sartre said, "We are condemned to freedom." Getting back on track, taking control of your life, means accepting *responsibility* for what happens in your life and the choices you make. It means embracing the freedom to process the events of your life in whatever way *you* choose.

Perhaps events have put you in the victim role. You need not see yourself as a victim. Perhaps you cannot change the devastating circumstances that have happened to you, but you can change the way you look at them. Are you fatalistic? Will this lot never be taken from me? Or—is this a temporary setback, downtime that in the future you will look back upon and say, "Well, *that* was a real character-building experience!" It's your choice.

You may choose to be a victim. But that choice is also a condemnation. You are deeding control of your life to others. You are allowing yourself to become a puppet with someone else pulling the strings.

Being free means ignoring the rules that aren't right for you. Have you always done things because it is expected of you? Are there traditions in your life in which you participate—and just *hate?* America goes through a mass migration every Thanksgiving. Does *everyone* really want to eat turkey with a relative?

Have you chosen a career or taken a certain job because it was what you "ought" to do? Ask yourself: are you playing by someone else's rules? If the rules are not your own, you will lose the game.

It's a bit like what happened to me when I was in Colombia to interview two of the survivors of the December 1995 crash of an American Airlines jet into the Andes Mountains. I was playing hide and seek with some children while the camera crew I was working with took a much needed break. We were playing, of course, in Spanish. My Spanish is not very impressive, but I was doing pretty well at being the seeker. Still—I lost miserably.

I was playing by the rules that I was familiar with. But these kids played the game differently. It wasn't enough to just find a child, you had to tag them too. And they were fast runners! The kids beat me every time.

Make sure that the strictures that guide your life are the right ones for you. If they aren't, unless you change the rules or change yourself, you will find success awfully hard to come by. It wasn't until I understood the rules these kids were playing by that I began to have any success with them.

Being free means risking the discomfort that comes with making a mistake. You might get messy. You may be given some excellent advice—and choose to ignore it. The lesson you'll learn from that error will not be forgotten. As someone wise once said:

The glory is not in never failing, but in rising each time you fail.

Analyze what happened, but don't be *paralyzed* by it. Pause to evaluate your life but don't get stuck in park. Sometimes the hardest part about making changes in our lives is not making the decision to change but taking *action*. This book is an example from my life. For a long time before I took the first steps, I imagined sharing the things I had learned as I got back on track from the *Today* show defeat. But it was a lo-o-o-ng time before I took any *action*.

Taking action requires more than just a hunch that this is the right thing for me. It requires a *belief*. It means you must move in the face of dozens of mental images (and perhaps "helpful" comments from friends and family!) about how and why you could fail.

Years ago, I came upon a realization that has made it much easier for me to make those tough decisions that I am sometimes hesitant to make. When seen in the light of this recognition, it has made decision making immeasurably less stressful:

There are only two acts in life that are not undoable: suicide and giving birth.

Think of this: except for suicide, which is obvious in *its* finality, and bearing a child (you might give it up for adoption, but somewhere out there is your flesh and blood), any action you might take, any decision you might make is rectifiable. There may be some pain involved, but if you marry and he's all wrong for you, you could divorce. If you take a job and it's horrible, you can quit. Paint a room and the color is just all wrong, you can do it over.

Identify what you might have done differently and resolve to *do it differently* if there is a next time.

Once you've completed your look back at what's happened, put what's happened away. File it away in your memory bank and leave it there. That's what helped tennis ace Monica Seles resume her incredible career. When Seles returned to the court more than two years after a deranged spectator stabbed her, she knew she had to segregate her thoughts about the attack or she'd never get her game back.

As she told an interviewer upon her return, "I've put the whole [stabbing] thing in a box. If I need to open it, I will, but I hope I don't have to."

Jana Stump sees the accident that paralyzed her as an experience she has put in a room in her mind. She can go there if she needs to, but the door is kept tightly shut.

I see the *Today* chapter in my life as one of the many file folders that I have put in my mental filing cabinet I can pull out if I need to. But aside from referring to the file for this writing, I try to keep it locked as much as possible. To be honest with you, even though I'm back on track, it still hurts.

Christina's analysis of her childbearing heartbreaks told her she'd fought as hard as anyone possibly could. There was nothing she could have *done* to bring that baby to term. The memory is one that is poignant and painful and carefully closed so as not to bring more tears in the future. Should she need to revisit it, she has the diaries that helped her get through the dark days. And when she rereads her diaries, she is reminded of just how far she's come.

Finish each day and be done with it.

You have done what you could.

For me, the epiphany in my recovery came—where else—on a plane. I was flying from New York to Los Angeles and was listening to the in-flight music channel. A song came on that seemed to hold me around the throat and demand I pay attention. It was a Jon Secada tune I'd never heard before. The lyrics grabbed me.

"I'm free. I'm free. Things are only as important as I want them to be . . ."

It has become my new motto. The defeats in my life do not have to define me—unless I allow them to.

I don't have to remain in mourning for what happened to me, unless I *choose* to.

If I don't make it important—it won't be.

Things are only as important as I want them to be.

No one can make what has happened to you in your past an issue in your life today . . . unless you let them. A failure can be a setback or a defeat. It's up to you, coach, to decide which it will be.

"Things past it is needless to blame."

—Confucius

The toughest thing about looking back is to do it in an emotional vacuum. When you've been hurt or shaken so profoundly, it is nearly impossible to examine the situation dispassionately. If you feel you were let down by someone, it is hard not to be angry. If life has dealt you a bad hand, it is natural to want to kick the card table over. It is easy to see that assigning blame might seem like the right thing to do.

Don't play the blame game. Blaming someone or something else assigns responsibility for your life to someone else. It removes the control and the ability to orchestrate where you will go and how you will feel about yourself to another party. You deserve better than that!

Chapter Ten

CHARTING YOUR COURSE

"If you see it, you can be it."

IF MY MOTHER WERE AROUND, this was the kind of morning that she would have been saying, "Why mothers grow gray!" Niki was being absolutely *impossible!* Whiny. Uncooperative. And though I was trying to be a nice mommy, I could feel my reservoir of patience getting dangerously low.

"Gr-r-r-r!" I growled to myself. "Here we are—on a ski vacation—and he is being a little monster!"

"I don't w-a-a-n-t to go skiing!" he wailed, as I tried to wrestle his snowpants on his legs while he tried to wriggle away.

"But Niki, this is the day you get to go race!" I figured the prospect of unlimited speed would be an inducement. After all, he'd talked of practically nothing but today's scheduled race at ski school since we'd picked him up the day before.

That only set him off more. The tears started flowing and the whining turned into full-blown sobs. I couldn't figure out what was going on.

"Niki," I asked as I hugged him to my chest. "What's wrong?"

"I don't want to go to ski school and I don't want to race!" He was screaming at the top of his lungs now. At this point, everyone in the condominium knew the day wasn't starting off well for one five-year-old.

"But angel, I thought you wanted to go down the race track." I kept my voice low and silently asked God to give me the patience I needed to keep from blowing my stack too. Back and forth I was rocking Niki as I talked.

Slowly the sobs started to subside.

"Mommy, I don't want to go to ski school." He was still crying, but at least he wasn't screaming.

"But älskling [which is Swedish for darling], why not?" I stroked his hair and kissed the top of his head.

"Because I might not win the race."

Ah ha! Now we had gotten somewhere. All the screams and the drama and the hysterics were symptoms of Niki's fear of failure. We all have it . . . but I honestly didn't think that a five-year-old wrestled with that same paralyzing feeling. He didn't want to go to ski school because he might lose the race. And in his childlike reasoning, Niki figured if he stayed home, his problem (losing) would be solved.

My mind raced like a computer. Now that I understood what the real issue was—how was I to deal with it? Had I unconsciously taught my son that winning is the only thing? Had I been so obvious about my disappointment in my own failures that I'd turned my own son into a tentative, hesitant little boy? In the next thirty seconds, I asked myself, how do I get him to understand that it's not the outcome but the journey that's important?

"Niki," I started, "it's not important whether you win or not. What matters is that you try your best and that you are smiling when you cross the finish line."

"But I might not w-i-i-n!" His voice wailed out the last word and I could see a new flood of tears was just around the bend.

I made Niki look me in the eye as I asked him if he was scared of not doing well and losing. The quiver in his bottom lip told me that was exactly the problem.

"You know what?" I said. "Sometimes Mommy is very worried about doing well. A lot of times Mommy has to do something that I'm not at all sure I'll do right. Like when I hit a golf ball or when I have to give a speech or even sometimes when I have to do my job at *In Addition*." Niki never has referred to my program by its proper name!

He looked at me. Those big blue eyes communicated wonderment that Mommy could *ever* be uncertain about *any*thing!

"And you know what I do?" I continued. "I imagine what it would be like to do it well and I try to picture myself hitting the golf ball the way I'd like to—and you know what?"

"What?" His voice was hopeful and expectant.

"I almost always do better than I thought I would—just because I imagined it." I tried to sound upbeat and enthusiastic.

It looked like my talk was working.

Niki stopped resisting and let me pull on his snowpants.

"And if you imagine yourself skiing well and crossing the finish line and having fun—I bet you will!"

It worked! Niki's lip stopped quivering and a smile started with his eyes and worked its way to his lips.

"Okay, Mommy—I'll try."

Later that day Karl picked Niki up from ski school. A bright pink ribbon was pinned to his parka—for winning, he told us.

Of course all the children got ribbons—there were no winners or losers. But in Niki's mind, he was a winner.

"Daddy, guess what!" he excitedly told Karl. "I won! And you know what? I won because Mommy said I would."

That wasn't exactly what I'd told Niki. But in his mind—if he imagined and believed it—it was true.

STEP NUMBER NINE TO GETTING BACK ON TRACK: VISUALIZE YOUR FUTURE

The path you've been traveling has given you some hard knocks. It's left you afraid to enter that race because you might not win. Now we're going to plot a course that will get us through the race of life—successfully.

Susie may not be able to erase the diagnosis that has broken her heart and changed the course of her sons' futures. But she can guide her sons and her family down a path that will bring them happiness and joy—and make the unchangeable sadnesses that the future will bring a little easier to bear.

Just the other day, she made a big step toward doing that. In looking ahead to the future and trying to get a handle on how the family can keep active with their sons as their physical needs become greater, Susie recognized she was looking past the more immediate possibilities.

"I met this guy in a wheelchair at the place where we were having our van converted and he's traveled all over the place. And hearing him, I realized that Florida and California are no-brainers as far as handicapped travel goes. We can go to California when we have all this stuff to lug around. *Now's* the time we should go to Europe to ride in a hot air balloon!"

Susie can't bring herself to visualize her future in anything more than the blurriest of scenarios. The doctors have told her how muscular dystrophy progresses. It is a picture Susie almost physically pushes away. "I figure when I'm there, I'm there. By the time the boys are about to die, it will be time for them to die . . . " Her eyes well up with tears. "And," she sniffs, "I will want them to and that makes me sad."

The inevitability of her sons' disease hangs like a canopy over Susie Albert. There are times when every day brings new challenges. She's not always sure she can rise to them. One of those came last night when she was made aware of just how much her older son, Jack, knew and understood about his disease. It was knowledge that he had gained through the cruel comments of a former nanny who had cared for the children.

"I didn't realize just how much of all of this Jack gets," Susie explained. "But last night he told me what this nanny we'd had for a long time had said to him. Things like, 'You know, the reason your father is not home that much is because you have muscular dystrophy and he doesn't want to be around you.'"

Susie's voice rises in anger as she continues, "I don't know what made her think she could say something like that. So every time his father has gotten mad at him or something's wrong, Jack immediately thinks 'It's because he doesn't love me because I have MD.' That is the absolute worst because you never want a child to feel that way!

"And then he said to me, 'Mom, she also told me there would never be a cure for muscular dystrophy.'" Tears are now spilling from this pained mother's eyes. "And that's tough . . . " Susie pauses and sniffles. "What do you say to that?

"You don't want them to have suffered and it's obvious he *has* suffered. It's amazing how well he's done considering what this woman said. I never knew about any of this until last night."

A tear falls down Susie's cheek. "It's amazing to sit and talk to Jack like I did last night . . . and, and . . . know that he's my best friend." For a rare moment, the heartbreak of the Albert family is laid bare. There is nothing this mother can do to change her sons' futures. And that is achingly, wrenchingly sad.

Susie is silent for a few moments. Then she speaks. "Certain things you just have to stay away from." Taking a deep breath, she continues. "I'll probably feel a whole lot better for the next few weeks because I got that out. Maybe that was bothering me."

As much as she might hope to, Caye Allen knows she can't change the events of April 19, 1995. All the prayers and hopes in the world can't put the Murrah Federal Building back together. None of the deals one might make with God will have Ted Allen safely back at his desk. Caye knows that, and in accepting that truth she has opened her heart to some astonishing assurances that she and her children will be okay.

"I feel like he's watching out for me," Caye told me. "You're going to think this is really strange, but one Sunday morning I was standing in the kitchen wearing one of Ted's T-shirts that I always slept in, and I felt this little tug on my shirt.

"I thought, 'Well, Austin's gotten up.' And I turned around and he wasn't there and I thought, 'Well . . . okay.' And I went back to what I was doing. A few minutes later, I was turning some bacon over and then I felt it again! Another little tug on my T-shirt. I swear to God it scared me to death . . . and then I thought, 'What are you scared of?' "

When they'd cook breakfast on weekend mornings, Ted and Caye often teased each other. Ted used to always give Caye's T-shirt a little tug. She turned around and looked. Again, there was no one there.

Later that day, she had another experience that gave her the very clear sense that her husband was still with her. "I was in the kitchen again, loading some dishes in the dishwasher, when I smelled Aramis, which was Ted's cologne.

"And I thought, 'Dang it, Austin's gone back there and sprayed that Aramis on him!'

"And so I called, 'Austin!' No answer.

"'Austin!' I really yelled his name," Caye continues. "And finally he comes from the back of the house. I said, 'Austin, were you just in here?' And he said, 'No.'

"I said, 'Come here.' And I made him come over so I can smell him. There was no cologne on him!" Caye finishes the story with a bit of amazement in her voice.

"Things like that happen all the time," she says with a smile.

It is possible that somehow Ted Allen has sent his wife signs of his love and lingering presence? Who knows? But enough odd occurrences have been noticed by Caye and some of her children that they believe Ted's comforting presence is still with them. And that has helped the Allens get back on track.

"I believe that he can hear me. I believe that he can see me. He can see what's going on." Caye is emphatic. "And Austin believes that too."

In fact, the Disney story of another son who lost his father has been a great solace to young Austin, who was only four when his dad was killed. One night after the funeral, Austin took one of his older brother's friends out to the backyard. He wanted to show her something. A star. The North Star.

Austin calls it his Daddy's Star. Just as Mufasa told Simba in *The Lion King,* "I'll always be with you," Austin believes as long as he can find that star in the night skies, his dad is with him.

Some would ridicule such notions. For the Allen family, they've provided the fuel to keep themselves going forward.

"Change your thoughts and you can change the world."

—Norman Vincent Peale

They say we use only 4 percent of our brain power. It seems to me, that bit of brain power we *do* use we often use in ways that don't make our lives any easier.

There is a growing body of scientific research that supports the notion that we *can* psyche ourselves up as well as out.

Years ago, when Joyce Summey was helping me get ready for the Junior Miss pageant, I believe she very quickly came to the re-alization that this kid is scared to death at the idea of competing with girls around the country. She was right. I had only entered the contest as a lark. My friends were doing it, so I did too. None of us actually expected to win!

Again, Joyce had a commonsense trick to help me get over my considerable stage fright. She told me, "Before you walk out on that stage, before you go out to say a word, take a moment and think about how well prepared you are. Think about how well you are going to do. And think about all those people sitting there say-ing to themselves, 'My! Isn't she something! I'm glad we saw this!'"

I have to admit, it seemed like the *dumbest* thing in the world to do.

Even though I'd practiced looking cool, calm, and collected, I sure didn't think I'd mastered that. And when your talent is sewing as mine was, what you imagined the audience saying is something along the lines of "That poor child, she just doesn't know how to do *anything!*" I'll be honest, it was a talent presentation that didn't exactly seem in the same league as the girl from Utah who sang an aria from La *Bohème!* But with the addition of a few magic tricks and some flash pots that exploded on stage, I was able to model four or five outfits I'd made and get through the three minutes we were required to fill.

I was scared to death to march on that stage, but I had to. So, figuring I'd be humiliated anyway, I decided to give Mrs. Summey's trick a try.

It *worked!*

I not only was able to walk out there—I actually had *fun* on stage. I didn't come close to winning, but instead of it being total torment, participating in the pageant turned out to be a gas. And, it was being exposed to the television production team at Junior Miss that got me interested in television as a profession.

It's an interesting mind game—but does it have any basis in fact? Psyching yourself into walking on stage is one thing, but is there a corollary that really helps in *life?*

Having seen how thinking positively had made a difference in my own life, I wondered if others had been similarly helped. I started digging through medical and scientific journals and was surprised by some of the evidence I found.

Pediatrics magazine reported on research done through the University of New Mexico with mothers of premature infants. The mothers understandably wanted to provide their babies with natural breast milk, but the stress and anxiety of having their babies in intensive care adversely affected the flow of their milk.

Researchers worked with one group of mothers with a combination of relaxation techniques and visual imagery exercises on twenty-minute tapes. After one week, the milk production of the mothers who listened to the tapes was one and a half times that of the mothers who didn't get the cassettes.

"No man is happy who does not think himself so."

—Publius

When you look at the proverbial glass, do you see it as half full or half empty? Your outlook may play a role on your overall health.

In 1946, a study was begun with recent graduates of Harvard University in which ninety-nine men were given an open-ended questionnaire to complete. Based upon how they responded to the questions, they were ranked on their "explanatory style," the way they explain the bad things that happen to them.

Perhaps one person would see a negative event as a one-time occurrence, while someone else would see this as a long-lasting problem that will never go away. An event might be seen as having no bearing on one person's life, while the next guy thinks it will ruin everything. Finally some would explain events as internally caused—"it's me"—while others would point to an external cause.

Those twenty-five-year-olds whose explanations tended to be pessimistic: "It's me, it's never going to change, it'll ruin everything . . . " were *much* more likely to have poor health by midlife than the optimistic explainers. Beyond that, the pessimists tended to be poor problem solvers, to be socially withdrawn, and even as young people more prone to colds and the flu.

We've all read the magazine articles about patients with terminal illnesses who credit miraculous cures to their positive mental outlook. Those stories always bothered me because I was afraid that some critically ill person might read the article and fall into depression, thinking, "Well, if I were more cheery I would be cured! My disease is *my* fault."

That's too much baggage to put on anyone—healthy or ailing. However, there *is* a growing body of medical literature that points to a weakening of the immune system during periods of stress. Remember those husbands of breast cancer patients we talked about earlier? Their immunity to illness was significantly lowered after their wives passed away.

And on the flip side, *knowing* where you stand and *believing* you are going to make it result in positive physical changes in the body. Researchers studied four groups of Israeli soldiers on fast-paced twenty-kilometer marches (with heavy backpacks) to see how one's thoughts could influence the body.

Each group of soldiers was given differing information about the march and how close they were to completion. The researchers were testing the notion that knowing the end is in sight makes the pain more tolerable. Along the way and again twenty-four hours after the march was over, the soldiers' blood was tested for endorphins (the hormones that act as a painkiller) and for prolactin and cortisol (hormones that indicate elevated levels of stress and anxiety).

One group of soldiers was told to prepare for a long twenty-five-kilometer march but at the fourteen-kilometer marker, they were told the march would be much shorter than the twenty-five kilometers they'd been warned about. This group did almost as poorly as the group of soldiers who were not given any information about the march. Some of those soldiers dropped out and all of them had high levels of the stress hormones in their bloodstream.

The second best performing group had been told they would be making a fourteen-kilometer march. But at the thirteen-kilometer marker, they were told they would have to go an additional six kilometers. Even though they marched about the same distance as the group who'd been given no information, they did *better* because they had some *expectation* about what lay ahead.

And who did best? The group that was regularly told along the way how far they had gone and how much further they had to travel to completion. They had a goal and they were regularly apprised how close they were to meeting it.

I have observed that a life directed to an aim is in general better, richer, and healthier than an aimless one.

Still got your little notebook handy? It's goal-setting time. We've reached the point to start looking ahead to the good times to come. We're going to come up with a plan that will make them happen. It is time to start planning your tomorrows.

> *"After all, tomorrow is another day."*
>
> —Scarlett O'Hara, in *Gone With the Wind,* by Margaret Mitchell

You've got to hand it to Scarlett O'Hara. The woman never seemed to think ahead about anything. She was always putting it off to "think about tomorrow." And of course, when tomorrow came around, she used her charm and her cunning and her street smarts to get through whatever disaster was occurring. I guess in fiction you can be like that—but it just doesn't work that way in real life.

Of course, some things you just can't plan for. How could Susie have imagined there was a single mutated gene coursing through her body? How could Marcia have guessed a lunatic was stalking waiting to attack her? Their crises make my own career transformation from Golden Girl to goat seem totally insignificant. Yet—how on earth would anyone prepare for any of these things?

Some things you just *can't* prepare for, no matter how much advance planning and thinking you do.

When I was a student in journalism school, I'd long thought about what it would be like to report my very first television news story. But do you think in my wildest imagination I would have ever predicted that my cameraman would start smoking a joint on the way to our story? Yup! Here I am, nineteen years old—thrust unexpectedly into my very first news story. (Okay, I know the families of the De Kalb County, Georgia, Fire Department getting together for a picnic wasn't earth-shattering news, but heck, it was gonna get me on television!)

And what happens? My photographer starts smoking marijuana while he's driving to the assignment. The University of Georgia Journalism School does not tell you how to deal with reefer-toking camerapersons! What could I do?

Well, first, I prayed, "Lord, please, *please* don't let me get busted!" Then, I rolled down the windows and did what I could to fan the obnoxious smoke out the window. What I should have done was tell the idiot to put the dang thing out. But I was scared to death to cross anyone. Besides, this was my first story. Maybe that was what all creative people did to get ready for their assignment ("Did I really belong in television news?" I found myself asking).

There are some things that you cannot anticipate in life. Some things that happen that are simply so bizarre, they aren't to be imagined.

But not many.

I was speaking to a group of ladies in Raleigh, North Carolina, not long ago. They were attending a conference designed to help them in their careers. It was a symposium of workshops on managing meetings, strategizing, and positioning oneself within the corporate environment. This was one together bunch of gals.

I asked them, "How many of you think out an important business conversation *before* you have it? How many of you think of what you will say and try to anticipate the other party's response? If they say this, I will counter with that. If they say that, I will counter with the other." Well, you know the answer—every hand in that room went up.

And it makes sense. I never ask a question on live television if I don't have a pretty good idea of what the person's going to say in response. At *Inside Edition* I usually chat a couple of minutes beforehand with anyone we're interviewing live on the show.

At *Today,* we were always presented with what we called a "preinterview." A segment producer will chat with the guest on the phone before they appear on the program and type up the questions they are asked and the answers they gave in the preinterview. It reduces the risk of surprises and helps the interview segment go much smoother.

They say a lawyer never asks a question if he doesn't know what the answer will be. At least that's what they used to say before prosecutor Chris Darden asked O.J. Simpson to try on those gloves during the murder trial. How much smoother the prosecution's case would have been without that courtroom gaffe. Jurors would have been denied one event that could raise a reasonable doubt about the ownership of those gloves. And Johnnie Cochran would have been denied the poetic "If it doesn't fit, you must acquit" mantra of his final argument.

And yet, when I asked those ladies in Raleigh—all of whom prerehearse any important work conversation—how often they do the same thing with their *life,* most of them just looked sheepish. I didn't ask for a show of hands on that question—I knew there would be plenty of embarrassed people whose hands would be remaining in their laps!

You've heard it said a zillion times. They make posters with the slogan, "There is no dress rehearsal in life." And yet we never write ourselves a script to go by.

Too many of us meander through life without any real plan or program for how we want our lives to proceed. Our goals are vague or merely event-specific. "I want to get married. I'll get a degree in psychology. When I save $20,000, I'll make a down payment on a house."

"Going the wrong way? God allows U-turns!"

—Church sign in Dalton, Georgia

If you don't like the way your life is going, change it! If you don't like the direction you're headed, switch course. But before you can do that, you must know where you are headed.

Earlier in this book, you learned who you are by spending some time in quiet reflection. You've focused on what you believe in, what you find important. You discarded that which you find irrelevant and got reacquainted with the people and pursuits that make your life rich and meaningful.

VISUALIZE YOUR FUTURE

If you see it—you can be it. If you believe it, you can become it.

You may not be very happy with some part of your life or perhaps all of your life in general. It seems to me you have two choices: you can do nothing and be miserable *or* you can make the changes that will make you feel more joyful about your life, your career, your family.

Again, I'll ask you to do the difficult. Find some more time you can claim for yourself. Farm the kids out, skip lunch, and go to a quiet place (try the research stacks at the library—no one is ever there at lunchtime), get up really early before the rest of the household. Find a place where you can think reflectively and give yourself enough time to do it.

Ask yourself: "Am I happy with my life the way it is today? What would I like to see different about my situation, about the way I feel?"

If you are feeling stressed, try to pinpoint the source of your tension. Are you being asked to do too many things and just don't have enough time to do it? Ask yourself: Are you really being asked to do these things, or are you taking them on yourself because you are "Superwoman" or it's a "woman's responsibility." If so, as you contemplate, think: delegate.

Is your marriage in a shambles? Do you want to save it? Is he unwilling to change? When Michelle Weiner-Davis published her book *Divorce Busting,* she was a guest on my radio show. She talked about her commonsense advice to spouses troubled by the state of their marriage. She advocates that *you* change. Even if he doesn't move an inch, the marriage will be different by virtue of the laws of physics. For each action, there is an equal and opposite re-action. If *you* react differently to a situation, if you don't take the bait when he's picking a fight, if you take charge in areas in which you previously let him take the lead—*he* will respond in ways he never did before. He has to. The dynamics of the situation are changed. Reacting in the old ways will no longer be appropriate.

As you sit quietly, ask yourself: What are your dreams, what goals remain unrealized? How important are they to you? Is your work fulfilling or simply a paycheck? In that picture-perfect world called your imagination, how do you spend your days?

Write your life vision down. Then study it and as necessary when you review it, make modifications or additions to your vi-sion. Next separate the fantasy from the attainable.

This is the beginning of your life's road map. I can hear some of you muttering under your breath at me, "Give me a break, Deb-orah, none of this stuff is going to happen just because I write it down."

That's right, just writing it down won't get you one bit closer to achieving it. But it can help you focus on where it is you ought to be going. Putting your life vision on paper won't automatically put you where you want to be, but it's a start in that direction.

"If one advances confidently in the direction of his dreams, and en-deavors to live the life which he has imagined, he will meet with a success unexpected in common hours."

—Henry David Thoreau

Remember those tiny baby steps we took when we were first trying to get over the initial shock of our crisis? You're now going to map out the baby steps that will help you travel straight to the kind of happiness you have imagined for yourself. And your "Life

Vision Statement" will be your guide.

Your Life Vision Statement should be a broadly sketched plan that will help serve as your road map. As you get stronger, you will probably find you will want to revise it. My original Vision Statement only pictured me feeling good about myself again. The career and family parts of the picture emerged later.

Your Vision Statement will show your goal and give some hints how to reach it. But there is more than one way to reach your goal. Just as a road map offers many different ways to get to Point B from Point A, you should be flexible in how you look at your Vision Statement. What initially seems like the surest and most direct way to a destination can sometimes be the least rewarding.

How many times have you veered off the Interstate highway to take the back roads? Chances are you made some wonderful discovery and captured some special memories.

Years ago, Karl and I were having one of those great vacations with no timetable, no real agenda, *and* no hotel reservations. We ended up in a little town where the best place to have lunch was beside a stream with bread and cheese from the local deli and wine chilled in the creek. It was one of the best moments of that trip—and completely unexpected. Have a life vision—but be prepared to look for the interesting way to reach your goals.

Don't be locked into your Life Vision Statement. Long before she experienced any of her fertility problems, Christina planned her future. When she was eight or nine years old she drafted a document she called: "My Plan." The goals are dear in their childish simplicity.

1. Graduate from high school and attend a four-year college
2. Drive a station wagon like the neighbors
3. Have four kids
4. Get married

It may be that Christina had the order a bit askew, but she

managed to achieve all of her childhood goals. All but one. She has now revised her "My Plan" to include some of the new goals and challenges she sees for herself.

Before you attempt to write a Life Vision statement, do a little thinking about what you want it to say. Think about your priorities: personal, family, community, professional. Look at your personal economics: is money a constant concern, is the presence of money a burden? Would striving for less in your life bring other, more meaningful, rewards?

The weeks and months following Marcia's rape found her in deep reevaluation of her chosen career. She'd gotten a job as a television reporter and even at this early stage in her career had won some impressive awards. But the prospect of a future in television was troubling to her.

"I no longer felt comfortable in my skin," she explains. "Most people [after a rape] retreat into their jobs, but I could take the least comfort from that . . . because of this person saying he watched me."

The more Marcia considered how uncomfortable she'd become as a TV reporter, the more she recognized that the stories which held the greatest interest for her were those which dealt with government service agencies. She began to refocus her earlier life vision.

"I'd always had an intellectual interest in this field and the rape drove me in that direction a little bit. I think much of it was that I thought in that arena I could avenge the wrongs done me.

"My attack has been one way in which it has been an inspiration for me to do something socially useful. It contributed to my feeling that television was becoming something dirty and unseemly. It was the ultimate statement that my participation in television was in no way a good thing."

When Marcia left TV, she went on to a career that has included work with children in need of supervision.

Focus, as Marcia did, on the crisis from which you are trying to recover. Use the thought starters which follow to help you chart your way and figure out which baby steps will help lead you to your goal.

Career Dilemmas:

- What job would you like?
- Is training needed?
- Talk to three people who do it.
- Research the field.
- What skills am I lacking?
- Are there related fields?
- Why is my current job wrong?
- What aspects of a different job appeal to me?
- Are there downsides? Change in locale, hours, salary?

Marriage Trouble:

- What do we argue over?
- When do we argue most?
- Imagine your life (in detail) without him.
- What was part of our lives in the beginning, that is missing today?
- Could I be happy without him?
- How could I change that would help the situation?
- What do I still like about him? (Tell him! It surely can't hurt the situation!)

Self-Image Issues:

- Are the roles I play right for me?
- Am I isolating myself?
- Am I trying to change my perceived flaws?
- Would counseling or a course be helpful?
- Go back and reread your self-esteem exercises.

Health Issues:

- Have I got all the necessary information?
- Which questions still nag at me?
- Do I have confidence in my doctors? (Remember, trust your gut!)
- Do I have moral support in place?
- Who do I know who has gone through a similar situation?

This is by no means an all-inclusive list of questions, but just some starters to help get your thoughts channeled as you plot out your course.

There is more than one way to get to where you want to go.

Having a life vision is important in reaching your goal, but what are the chances the plan you've mapped out on paper and in your head will *really* happen? Be honest!

I know you're thinking positively. You've eliminated the negative . . . gotten rid of the "n'ts" that held you back before. But face it, those curveballs are still likely to come your way.

Don't lose hope if you don't make it the first time. Thomas Edison tried two thousand different times before he successfully invented the lightbulb. Just because he failed more than 1,900 times, he didn't give up. He *believed* he would reach his goal. Those beliefs don't work just for the benefit of would-be famous inventors. They can work for you too.

Some scientists say the higher one's degree of hope, the greater the likelihood one will achieve one's goal. A study tested college students at the University of Kansas to determine the degree of hope with which they viewed goals. It was ultimately found that the student's degree of optimism was a better barometer of whether he would do well academically than were more accepted indicators, like test scores.

The research went even further. It found that the more optimistic students (the high-hope students) set higher goals for themselves, tended to believe that they would reach those goals—*and,* despite early setbacks, actually got the higher grades. The study found the high-hope students tended to focus on success and see their accomplishment in a more positive light than those with the less hopeful outlook.

The keys to the hopeful outlook? The hopeful students all had a determination to meet their goals, *and* they had a sense that they knew how to get there.

Ruth Brody believes that the hope that she can make a difference has been an important component in both her recovery from breast cancer and the redirecting of her life.

When Ruth closed her import business during her chemotherapy, she soon found the cost of continuing her insurance coverage skyrocketed to over $900 per month. With a number of surgeries looming on the horizon, there was no way she could let the insurance lapse, but the bills for medical coverage were sapping her financially. After many worried weeks of searching, she finally located a state-funded insurance program which would cover her. But even that wasn't cheap: it cost $700 a month.

Today, Ruth chairs a committee working as advocates for affordable health insurance. She now can be regularly found lobbying Illinois legislators to pass laws making affordable insurance available to everyone.

This is what your Life Vision Statement is all about: giving you a goal, the determination to reach it, and a concrete sense that these actions will get you where you are headed.

This may be the hardest step you'll take in your journey to get back on track. I know, some of the earlier exercises have *not* been easy. Now I'm asking you to stare into the wild blue yonder of your future and find a vision. It is like looking into the woods on a moonless night and trying to make out the scenery. You *know* something is there. But it is nearly impossible to discern what it is.

You *know* there is a plan for your life. You know that you can be the plan's architect. You've heard stories of women who've gone through some pretty amazing tragedies talk about their new life visions. You've seen some science to bolster the common sense of having a Vision Statement. But writing it? Whoa! Where do we start filling in the blanks?

WRITING A LIFE VISION STATEMENT

Start with *long-range goals:*

Five years from now, where do you see yourself personally and professionally? What do you envision being different in your life? If love and happiness are your ultimate goals (as I believe they are for most of us), what is it that will make you feel you have attained them? If financial security or professional success are your goals, what's needed to bridge the gap? Write it down.

Then subcategorize your goals into the steps needed to achieve them. If you lack the training or contacts or finances to take those steps, subdivide even further to include the actions you must take to address those deficits.

By working backward from your goal, you should come close to where you are today. It's a bit like following a family tree. Eventually each person who traveled on the *Mayflower* leads down many, many generations to someone who is around today.

Here's an example of a Life Vision Statement Ruth Brody might write to guide her in her desire to make a difference to breast cancer patients:

A: Goal:

Help focus breast cancer research.

B: What I need to achieve it:

Influence how cancer studies are directed.

C: And the steps to get there are:

Get on study commission advisory boards. Through her research, Ruth has discovered that very few breast cancer study
advisory boards have laypersons or cancer patients as members. But she has also learned that the average layperson or
cancer patient, while well intentioned, does not possess the
medical knowledge to be an effective member of such a
board.

D. I won't be able to accomplish C unless:

*I become educated as to how funding decisions are made and
get a basic background of the scientific issues involved.* Ruth
has taken an intensive scientific course that will teach her what
she needs to know to be eligible to serve on such boards and
be an effective advocate.

Mapped out, the process might look something like this:

A. Goal:

To achieve A, I must B: _____

The roadblocks to reaching B are C: _____

_____

Which means I will have to do D: _____

_____

As you look at your Life Vision Statement, you must *know* that
you can achieve it. If your vision finds you living in a home ruled
by peace and harmony (and it isn't that way now), focus on that vision. If your husband's doing something that you know is designed
to start an argument, don't take the bait. When the children drive
you to the point that you want to throw them all out the window,
do your ten-count relaxation exercise and let your blood pressure
lower.

You have the tools to make your vision a reality. Use them!

Yes, it is hard to let go of the hurt and anger and fear that are still lingering after your crisis. It is natural to find yourself occasionally drifting back to the wrongs you endured. You will still sometimes see the cloud of depression coming over the horizon. But you *cannot* focus on it. When it happens, practice the thought stopping we talked about in Chapter 4.

Remember, the more time you spend focusing on what you *don't* want, the less energy you are expending to achieve what you *do* want. Focus on what you want, and you have a map to help you get there.

And also remember:

"The world stands aside to let anyone pass who knows where he's going."

—Davis Starr Jordan

Chapter Eleven

FINDING A PURPOSE

"To every thing there is a season, and a time to every purpose under the heaven."

—Ecclesiastes 3:1

IT WAS A TYPICAL NEW YORK kind of day. I was running late, as usual. Couldn't find a taxi, as usual. And—as usual—my list of to-do items was way too long to be accomplished in the course of one day. And so naturally, when I pressed the elevator button, I had to wait what seemed like an eternity for it to arrive.

That's when Anna slipped through the door to speak with me.

"I just wanted to tell you," she said in a low conspiratorial voice, "that in my previous job, I was going through something similar to what you had happen to you at the *Today* show."

Anna worked for one of the top young designers on Seventh Avenue. She had one of those "front row center" kind of jobs that put her right in the middle of one of the more glamorous businesses in New York City. I couldn't imagine that her job was anything but tremendously exciting and rewarding.

She continued, "It was just horrible. There were days when I really didn't think I could go in there and put up with all the crap they were putting me through. But I'd see you on TV every morning and read what they were saying about you in the papers. And yet, there you were on the screen, just doing your job.

"And I'd say to my husband, 'If Deborah can get through it, so can I.'" She paused before she continued. "You were my role model during that time and it really meant a lot to me."

What could I say?

I was dumbfounded that anyone a) knew the pain that I was going through every day, and b) was actually benefiting from it.

I mumbled some sort of thank-you or something probably stupid and stumbled into the elevator stunned with the beginnings of a realization: This was *why* it all happened!

All along . . . during those days when I would say good morning to a colleague and be greeted with an icy stare. On those days when another "unnamed" staffer was quoted as saying something ugly about me. Those times when an "accidental" computer e-mail would flash an unkind message through my file, I sustained myself with the mantra, "There's got to be a purpose. God *has* to have a reason for this."

I said it, but I only half believed it.

I'd been raised to believe there was a purpose in adversity—and for the most part, I'd been able to see some good in the negatives in my life. My mother's death had been devastating to me—but it meant that she was no longer in physical pain. My parents' divorce truly did rip my adolescent world asunder—but it forced us as a family to express our love for one another.

When I bumped into Anna in the elevator hall, it had been two years since I'd left *Today,* but I still hadn't been able to figure out a *reason* for any of the pain. Each slight was like a stab wound whose only purpose seemed to be to make me bleed.

And yet *now* I knew why. The pain *did* have a purpose. This book is the final result of that realization.

When I was muddling my way through the mess at NBC, I really was *muddling*. I didn't have the vaguest idea how to pick up the pieces. There was no *How to Rehabilitate Your Reputation When You've Been Tagged As a Schemer* book at the corner bookstore.

I now know after having talked to literally thousands of women who have silently endured crises of their own, *they* didn't know how to get through it either. They just . . . muddled . . . like I did.

> *"That which doesn't kill me makes me stronger."*
>
> —Nietzsche

It is a perverse truism, I believe, but we have to experience the downs in life to appreciate the ups. The sour to recognize the sweet. The dark to appreciate the light. And life's hard knocks do have an end beyond making bruises.

Remember when you studied steel making in school? The factory workers started with a plain old iron bar. But what happened when they ran it through the furnace? The extreme heat tempered the iron, strengthened it. The iron emerged at the other end of the assembly line as a piece of steel. It took a furnace to make it *really* tough.

As you look back on the journey you've been making toward getting back on track, can you see how strong you've become thanks to your adversity? Look back in the journal you've been keeping. See how much distance you have put between the mindset you had when you first put paper to pen—and the way you feel about yourself now?

Now use that newly discovered strength to find out the *reason* that you endured what you have.

STEP NUMBER TEN TO GETTING BACK ON TRACK: FIND A PURPOSE IN YOUR CRISIS

There are times when I feel a bit like an ambulance chaser—but in a nice way. When I see someone wrestling with a disaster in their personal life, I find I am drawn to them to try to offer what help I can. At first, I chalked up this missionary zeal to the novelty of feeling good again. I was excited about having come out the other end of that tunnel I was in. In some ways, I was like a kid who's just gotten a new toy and plays with it incessantly.

Now enough time has passed that I know that my actions are not driven by any sort of fervor. I have seen the light go on in people's eyes when I've suggested some of the things that helped me. I've been there when the veil of darkness lifted and that first tiny glimmer of hope crept in.

When a friend miscarried a baby, I shared some of my self-esteem techniques and tried to help her see that *she* wasn't at fault and didn't cause the loss of her baby.

When another friend found herself suddenly single, it made my heart nearly burst to hear her *laugh* about the fun she had trying to make a silly do-it-yourself project. She was absolutely engrossed in her undertaking and had a terrific time with it.

And when my friend Betsy received the devastating news that her father had only weeks to live, we cried together and we talked. It was painful and took me back to the loss of my own mother so many years ago. But Betsy told me it helped just to have me listen. That made me feel like I was doing a little good. And that felt nice.

"Make yourself necessary to somebody."

—Ralph Waldo Emerson

"I think I am meant to do something else," Christina now believes after trying so valiantly to have another child and being so

bitterly disappointed. "Either something my son is going to be involved in in a very great way and he needs my 100 percent support—*or* there is something *I* am meant to do on the face of this
earth that having another child of my own might have prevented
me from doing.

"I don't know *what* it is—but there's something."

Christina has found a soothing, healing peace in growing to
accept that more children probably won't be a part of her life. That
life plan she made when she was eight years old has been revised.
The vision of a houseful of children, while not a forgotten memory,
no longer haunts her.

She now goes through life with a hopeful expectation that
someday, perhaps soon, that new life purpose will be clear to her.
And she's actively taking steps to keep her eyes and ears and *mind*
open to whatever that purpose might be. She's reevaluating a
home-based business she and her husband have operated. Perhaps
it's been too much of a drain on their personal time together. She's
planning more active time with her son, no longer reticent to make
long-range plans because there might be a baby in the picture.

Jana's astonishing strength in fighting the demons, both mental and physical, which helped her achieve top honors in more
than one endeavor, has been noticed by more than just her fellow
contestants at the national Junior Miss competition.

"People have written me and told me how I have affected
them. They say, 'You've made a difference in my life,'" Jana relates
with deserved pride. "I was an outgoing person before my accident, but I felt like I had to become *more* of an outgoing person
because I could tell people had so many questions they wanted to
ask, but they were afraid to hurt me. They didn't know how to act
around me."

Jana may not have the full answer as to why this accident happened to her, but she has made some sense of her situation. "This
has happened for a reason and I'm going to make a difference in
some people's lives. I am in this chair and I am teaching people."

When the last big earthquake hit in California, it devastated
families and destroyed homes. But for one of my friends, the shake-

up, though terribly frightening, had some positive side benefits. Once the dust settled, they had a contractor come out to examine their house, which as far as they could tell looked just fine. In fact, he discovered some major internal problems in the furnace system. Unchecked, they could have spelled disaster.

Crisis is the earthquake that rattles the foundation of your life. It shakes up your beliefs—*and*—it may also loosen some old baggage that is hampering you from getting where you are destined to go in your life.

Crisis forces you to look inward. It makes you reexamine your life plans, your relationships, the choices you have made.

Crisis can be a force for positive change—if you let it. You must believe that there is a better tomorrow for you after these difficult todays. That requires *faith*. And faith demands the expectation of something even though there is no tangible evidence it exists or will ever come your way.

As a born-again Christian and wife of a minister, Cynthia Green had rock-solid faith in the Bible verse "All things work for the good of them that love the Lord." But when her husband, David, seemed to lose his life's direction, when their business collapsed taking their future inheritance with it, when the stock market went down the drain and nearly took her marriage with it, that belief was challenged.

"Was your faith a sustenance?" I asked Cynthia. "Or an anchor around your neck?"

"H-m-m," she thought a moment. "You worded that well. I think it haunted me. I was so angry. It was displaced anger. I didn't know where to put it, so I put it at God. I turned my back on God and to this day, nothing scares me more than to leave my rock."

Eventually, as Cynthia and David began to repair their shaken marriage, she began to rebuild her shattered faith. The couple began to attend worship together. They started getting involved at church and began spending time with their friends. David began working as a junior high guidance counselor and Cynthia found a position as a social worker. But as they began to get their chins above water financially, Cynthia got some depressing medical news: her wildly irregular periods meant it was highly unlikely she would ever be able to conceive. The stress of the Greens' financial troubles, their doctor suspects, may be a contributing factor to her health problems.

But all of these troubles forced the Greens to take off the blinders. A friend who serves as a foster parent once asked Cynthia to help her baby-sit. Eighteen-month-old John absolutely captivated Cynthia and David.

"He's just precious!" Cynthia coos. "He's got fat little chubby thighs and chocolate brown eyes and his hair is lightening up to a lighter brown. He weighs about twenty-eight pounds. If they had a baby division in the strongman contest, he would win!"

The Greens first became approved for weekend visits with the bouncy toddler. Then they became full-time foster parents. Cynthia believes the arrival of this very special child into their home is a part of the purpose of their crisis.

"We're still on that journey toward getting back on track, but I think that John is a part of the journey. Getting him into our home and into our lives is a miracle to me. For years, David had said, 'I can't be a father,' and then all my physical problems. But John is my miracle. I praise God because he is my joy and I think it's a part of . . . " Cynthia's voice has gotten weepy. "I'm sorry, I'm losing it," she sniffs.

"I think part of the reason why God moved when He did and told us to redirect our lives was because there are children who are in need."

The Greens are now hoping to become John's legal parents. Where once they prayed for success in business, today they are asking God to let them adopt this child.

Everything we have worked on during our journey toward getting back on track has led to one point: You've acknowledged the crisis that happened and taken steps to feel good about yourself again. You've given up the situations and people which make you feel pressured. You've learned to relax. You've looked back on your past, maybe found some mistakes you made—and you've written your life script to guide you as you go forward.

You are more together *now* than at probably any point in your recent past. If your crisis brings nothing more than that—what a terrific benefit you have gained! I'll bet you're saying to yourself, "Well, I'm paying a pretty high price just to get my act together! It has to be more than just *this,* but I'll *never* figure out what the purpose is!"

That may be, but it may also be that it's too soon for you to be able to see a deeper meaning. It has been just over a year since Robin's husband walked out and she began what she now knows will be a life alone. "I still can't say that there is a better purpose or that things will be better or that there is an interest in having suffered this pain. Maybe there *will* be something down the line and there will be a wonderful future . . . But no, I don't know if I could ever say there is a greater purpose that could make this better because what we had and could have had was better."

Robin has not yet been able to stop looking backward. She knows that her old married life is over. She can even admit that her old married life was far from perfect. But she cannot yet emotionally let go of her marriage. Like Lot's wife who ignored God's admonition not to look back at the evil village of Sodom and Gomorrah and was then turned to a pillar of salt, Robin is still looking back at her old life. And she is as emotionally paralyzed as a statue of salt.

"Look at this perfect, wonderful family," she sobs. "Yeah, Don and I weren't perfect, but when I look at the children, when I look at their unhappiness, at the things that we had . . . *how* can I say there is a better purpose?"

My guess is, one day Robin will find some meaning to the end of her marriage and that will take some of the sting out of her pending divorce. It won't happen anytime soon. Finding your purpose may be something that doesn't happen for years. It was at least two years after I left *Today* that I felt I could say this was the greater good to come of all the hardship. It's taken me even longer to put all this on paper.

Perhaps these questions will help as you try to *find a purpose:*

- What is different in your view of the world now?
- Do you handle situations in a way you did not previously?
- Do you find your focus on life's priorities is changed?
- Have you consciously or subconsciously steered your life in a direction you otherwise wouldn't have taken?
- What's better about you, your viewpoint, your attitude?

"One thing we've learned through all of this is not to pass judgment on any family." Christina knows that her thinking has certainly changed with respect to other childless couples she might know. "Don't think they are selfish. That they just want to spend their money on themselves, all their time on themselves. *Nobody knows* what that particular couple might have been through. I am much less judgmental!"

I find that my perception of people's situations is different too. Just as I sometimes act like a fire engine rushing to rescue those around me when their crises hit, I find myself looking back and regretting that I was not more supportive when people I was close to suffered losses. Oh sure, I went to the funerals and called friends who I knew were lonely. I wasn't a *bad* person. But I wasn't especially empathetic, either.

Somehow I'd been able to compartmentalize my own hardknocks of losing my mother and seeing my folks divorced—remember this is the former Golden Girl speaking—so that I didn't fully understand just how devastating their situations were to them.

I remember one phone call I made just after Niki was born. I called Leah, my old college chum—and I apologized. She had a two-year-old boy and her second son and Niki were actually expected on the same due date.

A few weeks after I had come to relish the joy and wonder of being a mom, I called Leah and said, "I am so sorry. So sorry that I did not properly acknowledge what a wonderful change you and

Dan were experiencing when Alex was born. I just didn't *know* how incredible this life change was. I wish I had celebrated better for you."

Leah was so wonderful. In that sweet voice I've grown so fond of over the last twenty years, she said, "You don't have to say you're sorry. You couldn't have known. There is no *way* you could have known how special this is. Now you do."

And perhaps that is also a part of the purpose I have found in my own crisis. While I hope some ladies going through their own rocky road read this and are comforted by what I and the other ladies here have said, some of this is directed at the persons who are like the pre-*Today* Debbie.

While you may not fully understand the depth of loss your friend might feel, I hope you will be better equipped to help them deal with it. That's what Joan has discovered.

"I am a different person than I was before. Some of that is very, very painful—and some of that is probably for the good."

"Are you a better person?" I asked.

"Yes, I am. I am much more in touch with other people's fears and sorrows. I realize now that even people who are unpleasant are probably acting that way out of some sort of pain or fear of their own. It's interesting. If you don't react to the anger on the surface but react to the emotion that's resonating underneath, it's amazing how you can bleed off the anger in somebody."

Joan put it in a context that anyone who's been around little kids can understand. "It's like they say about two toddlers and one hits the other. The one who needs to be comforted is not the toddler who was slapped, but the toddler who did the slapping. Because that is the toddler who's scared because they're out of control. That is the toddler you put your arms around and reassure."

Rebeccah can look now at the richness of her life and appreciate it. By making an effort to take a little time for herself she enjoys her roles as wife and mother. The bout with the blues that had momentarily crippled her had helped her come to this new, more satisfying point in her life.

Maybe these explanations don't make sense to you. Perhaps you read what some of these women believe the purpose of their crisis to be and say to yourself, "They're just kidding themselves!"

So what if they are? What is important is that they have discovered a meaning that is right for *them*. It doesn't matter if it is the *right* meaning. What is right in these matters is subjective anyway. *No one* can know if there is a grand plan to any of the occurrences in life.

Whatever the meaning given to what has happened in these women's lives, allows them to put it behind them—or at least aside—and get on with living. The sore may not be completely removed, but at least it's now in a place where it can't be reached and reinfected.

Even though years have passed since her assault, Marcia has not forgotten a moment of it. The memory has played constantly in her mind like a never-ending song. But as she has turned toward her new profession and her new life with the man who stood by her through the worst of it, the refrain has grown dimmer.

"It's as though someone is turning down the music. It keeps fading and fading. The sound is still there inside my psyche, but it's less noisy. Less bothersome."

The new life direction Marcia has found as a result of her crisis has helped her move on.

Epilogue

MOVING ON

"Just when you thought you had it figured out—things change."

WELL. THEY GOT ME AGAIN.

Here I am. Writing the final pages of a book that is supposed to be helping women get their lives back together again—and I've been sitting in my office crying!

I thought by now—six and a half years after it all began—the print press would have had its fill of ugly Deborah Norville stories. But, as Ronald Reagan would have said, "There they go again!"

I'm still stunned at where this one appeared: a *Ladies Home Journal* publication! Supposedly one of the better women's service magazines. It's really sort of amazing. Here they print a page that includes me among the "Women We Spent 1995 Loving to Hate"— and yet in that same year, 1995, the magazine's associate editor, Shana Aborn, had asked me to write an essay for them! I had to decline since I was under contract to *McCall's* (a competitor) as a contributing editor.

The blurb said in part, "Some staffers at *Inside Edition* . . . have even accused her of having her publicists send fan mail about her they had written themselves to *TV Guide*." I was described as "imperious and manipulative." And—just in case the article really *wasn't* true, it ended: "Whether the accusations are true or not, we're all growing weary of reading about Norville's misadventures."

I knew where this one had originated. The existence of the letters was printed in one magazine some time earlier, and of course the story didn't make me look very good. The woman who was the *Inside Edition* publicist when I joined the program had some laudatory letters about me addressed to *TV Guide* in her computer file. She admitted to the producers that she had written them herself. (A couple of questions: a) Why would someone do something like this? And b) Why would you put it in your office computer? If hackers can break into the government's computers, isn't it a safe assumption that the computer at work is penetrable?) The publicist told the bosses that "Deborah never knew about this"—and I assured the bosses that if I had known about such a stunt, I'd have put an end to it fast.

I was furious—for a lot of reasons. I couldn't imagine why anyone would do something I thought so silly as make up these letters. I was upset about the ugly comments the magazine made about me. And I was *very* distressed that no one at the office bothered to let me know about any of this. When the whole mess happened, I was on vacation with my family in Sweden visiting my in-laws.

"We didn't want to ruin your vacation," was what I was told. Well! It surely didn't make coming home very much fun!

Most of all, though, I was disappointed and frustrated that the company did not respond to the story. I argued for a statement explaining the whole mess, something that came to my defense.

The bosses said no. They didn't want to protract this thing in the press. (Does any of this sound familiar? As I was going through it all, it really was déjà vu. "Trust us, Deborah, we're experts at this . . . " echoing through my mind at the time.)

"Well," I recall telling my agent, bitterly disappointed, "I may have blonde hair and blue eyes and am therefore stupid, but I know something about this sort of thing. Mark my words—this won't be the end of it."

I hate to say, "I told you so . . . but . . . "

When I felt I had gotten back on track from the *Today* mess, one of my resolutions was to stand up for myself if I felt I was being unfairly attacked. I was still new at *Inside Edition* when that first article came out. I let the bosses handle it their way. But when I saw the item being reprised in the *Ladies Home Journal* piece, I knew I had to speak on my own behalf, even if no one else would.

I called Myrna Blyth, the editor-in-chief, to express my concerns to her directly. Her assistant said she had severe laryngitis and wouldn't return until the following week. I asked that she call me when she was back in the office.

Meantime, Lisa Dallos, the new *Inside Edition* publicist who was brought in to replace the letter writer (who had been let go), made some calls of her own to try to find out who had written the piece and edited the section in which the article appeared.

Neither one of us could get anyone to call us back.

So I called some lawyers.

There is a Supreme Court ruling that governs a lot of what we do in journalism. It's the *Times v. Sullivan* standard, which states that to win a defamation case, a public figure must not only prove the article is untrue, but also that it was published with a "reckless disregard for the truth." When I first heard of *Times v. Sullivan,* it was in the context that I as a reporter must use care not to violate that standard.

Yet here I am picking apart *Times v. Sullivan* to see if I, as a public figure, have a legal case.

Put ten lawyers in a room and you'll get ten different opinions. One lawyer said since the article accused me of unethical behavior by encouraging persons to fabricate documents and lie on my behalf, it was defamatory. And that the magazine's failure to solicit any kind of comment from me or *Inside Edition* could be seen as reckless disregard for the truth. Another lawyer said it's a difficult case at best.

What they all agreed was that using the courts to set the record straight would cost me a small fortune. I could initiate legal proceedings or I could fund my sons' college accounts. As much as the emotional me wanted to call out the legal dogs, my practical side knew what was the right action to take.

So I wrote Ms. Blyth a letter. I reminded her that the magazine has asked me to contribute to their publication and asked if it was my inability to comply that put me in the editorial doghouse? Since *Ladies Home Journal* is known in the magazine world to position itself as a purveyor of strong journalism, I decided to appeal to the lack of journalism in the item. Here's some of what I wrote:

> As you know, my degree is in journalism and I have practiced it for eighteen years, so it is second nature to me to (a) verify my information before I publish it in a story and (b) solicit comment from parties who are involved. As the named party in this item, I am quite surprised no one at *Ladies Home Journal* took the time to call.

I'd like to think my well-chosen words helped convince the magazine folks of the error of their ways and caused them to hang their heads in shame. What most likely happened was that my lawyer's cover letter scared the dickens out of them. He described it as not so much threatening, as menacing.

Within days of the receipt of my letter, the magazine's legal counsel was on the phone with my attorney, promising that I need have "no fear" of further negative coverage.

When I heard *that,* I felt like I'd scored the winning touchdown at the Super Bowl. For virtually the first time in my life as a public figure, I had stood up to what I considered to be an unfair article. I fended for myself and didn't get cut down in the process.

232

With a mix of pride and regret, I wondered what might have happened in my life if I'd stood up to some of those rumormongers earlier.

I suppose it was Pollyanna of me to think that the hatchet jobs on me would end just because *I* feel I've gotten back on track. I *know* it goes with the territory of my profession. But even in this most recent sting, I've found a purpose.

Coming as it has while I finish this book, this little wound reminds me that getting back on track is not a static thing. You don't "do it" and then be done with it. It is a constant life process. One ebbs and flows toward that feeling of being in charge. Of feeling in control.

Like the seashell which is buffeted by a wave toward the ocean and then dragged back to shore, there are moments when I feel like I am losing it.

Then I refocus myself. I remind myself of something that I recognized early on in my own crisis: professionally speaking it can never be as hard as it was then. I look at how far I've come. It makes today's setback seem eminently manageable. And when the next bump in the road happens, I'll be able to handle that too. Because it *will* happen.

In looking at the stories of all the women who have spoken with me about crisis, both for attribution in this book and just in conversation, I've noticed one thing we all have in common. We have lost our illusions. Not one of us harbors any fantasy that we've been dealt our share of bad cards and that from here on out the dealer's going to be sending us aces.

We are changed and now look at life with a view that is one part cynicism, one part optimism, and a very healthy dose of realism. We may hope for good things in the future, but won't be surprised when the bad times come our way. Most important, we know we can deal with them *successfully* when they happen.

"Even when you're on the right track, you'll get run over if you just sit there."

—Will Rogers

Have you ever ridden the little putt-putt cars at the carnival? My boys love them because they think they're really driving the car. In fact, they have about six inches either side of the center guide rail in which to steer. If you don't steer just so, the guide rail will jerk you back onto the path.

That's what I liken getting back on track to: a putt-putt roadway. You're motoring through life fairly well, when all of a sudden, you bang into the rail and get jerked around a bit. But if you've found a life vision for yourself, if you've discovered a purpose to the adversities you've been through, if you know who you are— that center guide rail will be there to get you headed back in the right direction.

And trust me, you'll hit the guide rail when you aren't looking. Reminders of what you've come through will come at the most unexpected times.

Last Christmas we took the kids and relatives to see the Christmas Show at Radio City Music Hall. Afterward, we strolled toward Fifth Avenue to window-shop and, of course, walked past the big tree outside Rockefeller Center. Thirty Rock is where NBC is located, and today the new *Today* studio overlooks the plaza. For just a flash, I felt that chill you get when your blood seems not to pump for an instant. I felt that momentary lump in my stomach. It was the creepy *Today* show feeling all over again. I shrugged it off—but it *was* there. "Funny," I recall thinking. "I really thought I was over all that."

Every so often when you think you have successfully put your past behind you . . . it sneaks up and slugs you in the face.

Many years after Marcia's assault, long after she thought she'd mostly put it to rest, she got the same reminder. She'd gone out with some girlfriends and they all decided to catch a movie. The film, *The Accused,* for which Jodie Foster won an Oscar, was playing and the other girls wanted to see that.

"I thought, I'm okay. I can live with this," Marcia recalls. The movie is the story of a young woman who is gang-raped at the local bar. Marcia wasn't as okay as she thought. "I completely fell apart. Luckily I was with close friends who took me into the bathroom and just pulled me back together. I didn't realize it would do that to me."

Fifteen years after her attack, Marcia says the event is still with her. "Even now, there are nights I wake up and I'm right there in the middle of it."

"Ask not that events should happen as you will, but let your will be that events should happen as they do . . . and you shall have peace."

—Epictetus

The crisis that crippled you won't go away. There will be tough times to come. But they no longer need dictate and control your life—unless you let them.

Last spring, when *Inside Edition* broadcast the show from Chicago, I got a chance to spend some time with Joan and baby Ben. He's grown into a handsome little boy who truly does radiate happiness. Or perhaps he reflects it. Despite all the hardships, tears, and trauma, Joan seems happy. And the peace and joy of *her* life is mirrored in her little boy.

I said to her, "You seem so together—like it doesn't hurt deep down inside."

Joan *is* together. The pain is still there, just less obvious. "What you do to heal," she says, "is you talk about it. Over and over and over again. Then, the more you talk about it, the more the words lose their sting. The emotion is still there. The sadness is still there just below the surface. It's always going to be a part of me. But I think people are drawn toward what is light rather than toward what is dark. And I've had enough time to experience a lot of light and love."

That light and love is what Susie Albert is trying to give her boys—every single day.

"To do the best for them," she says. "That is my focus. The unfairness of their disease just keeps coming at you over and over and over again. But then I'll go to graduation as I did last year when Jack got all the awards. He was the top of his class and had a big smile on his face. I thought, if you could give a child a day in their life—*this* is the kind of day you would give him."

A moment of joy can bring a lifetime of pleasure.

While some of us can move the shrapnel from our life-altering experiences away from our day-to-day lives, that is obviously something Jana Stump will never be able to do. The chair is an ever present reminder of that freak accident in high school.

And yet, she has found peace. "I've gone on with my life and I've even made *more* with my life than I would have if I hadn't gone through this situation. But the wheelchair is always a part of me. I don't think you ever get completely back on track. You get back on track over and over again."

When Jana made the Olympic team it was the fulfillment of a goal she had set for herself three years earlier. While no one had told her, "Don't get your hopes up," no one said, "I've got no doubt you'll make it" either. It was a solitary struggle that Jana waged and won on her own.

And the message to it? Jana says it is quite simple: Never give up. Never give in. "Just be the best that you can be. Take what you have been given and make the best of it. In the five or six years I've been in a chair, I have not come up against a thing that I cannot do."

With a berth on the Olympic team, Jana is moving on. "My big goal for the past three or four years was to make the Paralympic team. Now that I've made it I'm going to change my goal. I want to enter another pageant." Jana Stump wants to be Miss America. In my book, she already is.

"We can only be said to be alive in those moments when our hearts are conscious of our treasures."

—Thornton Wilder

Rebeccah is more vivacious and filled with zest for life than at any time in her recent memory. She is past her mini-depression. Focusing on the many gifts in her life has kept her from slipping back into that morass of gloom.

Christina has stopped counting days on the calendar to chart her fertility and is instead now counting the days to a dream vacation she, her husband, and her very precious five-year-old Jonathan will soon be taking. She has stopped pining for what might have been and is relishing *what is*.

Marcia is married to the wonderful and supportive man who rushed to her side minutes after her rape was ended. Bill's support and love and understanding have kept her on her feet all those times when flashbacks of the intruder would cripple her. They now have two beautiful sons whose school and athletic activities keep her calendar more than filled.

Linda and Gary Thomas watch with pride as little Marisa continues to prove the "experts aren't" as she grows in her ability to accomplish more tasks on her own. The child who "would never know who her parents are" lives in a world of great love and happiness.

Robin had been told by a friend who had also gone through a painful divorce to just hang on until the daffodils bloom. When the first flowers of spring appeared the year after Don left, Robin was overcome with the knowledge that she had made it this far. She knows there is a future for her—and even suspects it may be a great future. Most important to her now, she sees that her children are coming through this change in their lives with remarkably few scars.

Joan has found a man. "He is the dearest, kindest, most giving man I have ever met," she says. He is wonderful with little Ben. He validates Joan as a mother. Last Christmas, they were married. Ben was at his mother's side.

Ruth Brody has learned an astonishing amount in her studies and expects that soon she'll be assigned to a committee guiding breast cancer research. She is closer than ever to both of her daughters and can't wait for the day they marry and make her a grandmother.

The other day, Susie Albert found a man who could come to her home and help evaluate what changes they can make to better accommodate the boys' medical equipment. She'd been looking for this kind of consultant for months and finding him has been the kind of thrill one gets when the Fourth of July fireworks finale lights the sky. She and her husband are talking about taking the family to some of Europe's landmarks while the boys' ambulatory needs are still manageable.

Caye Allen has become even more absorbed in her children's school activities. The loss of her husband has been a reminder that life is fleeting. She doesn't want to miss a single game or school play.

Her children don't want her to miss out on life. The other day, Austin's kindergarten observed Donuts for Dads Day, when all the children's fathers come to school for a snack. Austin told his mom she might want to come. Caye asked him why. He told her she might find someone to date!

Cynthia Green is a mom. She and David are permanent foster parents for little John, and they've already cleared the first hurdle toward legally adopting him.

"For the first time in my life, I feel like I'm nesting," Cynthia told me one night after John was tucked in bed. "There's a baby across the hall, David is working, and I'm now running my own home-based business." Cynthia sighs contentedly. "I feel like I'm home—and it feels right."

Jana, who came home from the Paralympics with a bronze medal, is continuing her education at the University of Illinois. She's found a great way to deal with those few buildings that have a daunting number of steps in front of the entrance: she finds the cutest boy in the vicinity and asks *him* to carry her up the stairs. "It's a great pick-up line!" she laughs. Jana's a broadcast news major. She'll make one heck of a TV reporter.

And me? I'm still here. There's a sort of wicked pleasure in knowing that I am on the screen there, still haunting all those people who thought they'd never see me again. I never thought I'd do it. And looking back on the path that got me here, it still amazes me a bit.

But then, I don't look back very often. It hurts too bad. In fact, I put off until literally the last moment to go through my old *Today* era clippings to get the quotes you read earlier. I sat in my little writing room and sobbed as I reread those hurtful articles. I walked with a little cloud over my head for a couple of days afterward. I know the best way for me to look back is only to see how far I've come. Then I turn my face forward.

The future seems as limitless and as full of promise as it ever did. Maybe even more so. I have finally taken off the blinders. The road ahead is one of opportunity. It is filled with chances. Writing this book is one of them.

It's up to me to stick my neck out. And, I've no doubt, there are probably a few "experts" in the press waiting in the wings with a sword to cut my head off. I can already tell you what some will be thinking: Who does she think she is? It's not appropriate for a journalist to write such a personal book. She's stirring up dust piles that have been left alone for years. Well, let 'em talk. I can't worry about *them*.

What I worry about, no—*care* about, is you. If you've been

given the shaft by life, you don't have to hang on to it. Give it back. You do not have to be depressed if you choose *not* to be. You are not defeated if you do not wave the white flag.

You have within you a huge reservoir of strength and talent and abilities. You have worth. Unless you recognize it first, the world will never see it. I have tried to show you how to tap in to that reservoir. I've posed the questions. The answers you give will show *you* the path you should take toward what will bring peace and contentment to your life.

When something so dramatic as death or divorce, illness or unwanted life changes happen, we expect the cure to be every bit as dramatic. It rarely is. Healing a broken leg *is* tedious. It takes time. The physical therapy is not only boring, it is sometimes painful.

Some of the exercises I have given you are, I'll admit it, *really* boring! The process of getting back on track is painful. And no one can do it but you. But when it's over, *you* will be able to say with pride, "I did it myself."

Step by step. Bit by bit. You can restore those blocks that have been rattled from the foundation of your life. The crisis that shook you and the rebuilding you went through are now a part of your life. It is part of who you are. If you let it, it can be what strengthens you and helps protect you from more hurt in the future.

It can be the stuff that helps you reach your dreams. Years ago in school, we studied the American poet Langston Hughes. A bit of one of his poems has always stayed with me:

> *Hold fast to dreams for if dreams die*
> *Life's a broken unwinged bird*
>   *that cannot fly.*

Your dreams can be realities. They are the stuff that lead us through life toward great happiness. *Believe* that this trauma you've endured *has* a purpose. Find it and grab it with both hands.

Had my career not tumbled as it did, I'd probably still be getting up at three in the morning, stumbling through life sleep-deprived, interviewing people whom I'd later see and say "Nice to meet you." I'd have no recollection of some of the people I'd chatted with on national television.

I'd be away from my family when they got up in the morning and probably so cranky in the evening they'd wish I were gone. Being forced to rebuild myself and find a new professional life has freed me to make different choices. Having lived through my professional trauma, I was able to choose a job that afforded me more quality time with my sons and husband. And—I am *strong* enough to fight for that time when the inevitable pressures of the office try to steal some of that time away.

I've tried to project how my life would be if none of this had happened. What I see is a "good girl" who accepts any assignment without reproach, who follows the rules, who does as she's told. I see a family that suffers as a result. I'm still a "good girl," but I'm much more vocal when it comes to calling the shots.

I *am* free. Things are only as important as I want them to be. This has become the motto of my life. I feel at times like Superwoman. There are moments when I am so energized by the good things in life, so excited knowing that I turned a bad situation around and did it myself, that I am sure I can leap tall buildings in a single bound. That's usually when reality bumps into me again.

The difference now is—reality doesn't leave scars. I take a deep breath and calm down. I do a quick mental rundown of the strengths I have to help me along. I seek advice but use my own intuition as to whether to accept it or not. And—I go forward.

I let events happen as they do—and I have peace. I have gotten back on track. You can too.

Resources

$\mathbf{T}$HE FOLLOWING ARE OFFERED AS starting points for gathering information and support for a variety of situations. While this list is by no means complete, it should provide some possible sources of assistance and information.

Adoption

THE NATIONAL ADOPTION CENTER   **800-862-3678**

They can provide information on adoption agencies, adoption support groups, etc.

Alzheimer's Disease

ALZHEIMER'S DISEASE EDUCATION AND REFERRAL CENTER   **800-677-1116**

Sponsored by the National Institute on Aging, this "Eldercare Locator" number can provide referrals to area agencies on aging, answer questions, and provide information on helpful publications.

THE ALZHEIMER'S ASSOCIATION   **800-621-0379**
    (In Illinois, 800-572-6037)

This group can provide general information about the disease and referrals to local support chapters who can offer local information regarding the disease and local care providers.

Alcoholics Anonymous

SEE LOCAL DIRECTORY.

Local chapters in most cities and towns in America. The only requirement for membership is a desire to stop drinking.

Breast Cancer

Y-ME BREAST CANCER SUPPORT HOTLINE   **800-221-2141**

Staffed by breast-cancer survivors, this number offers supportive counsel to breast-cancer patients, patient information, and outreach for patients and families.

Cancer

AMERICAN CANCER SOCIETY   **800-227-2345**

Information on cancer issues and counseling for patients and family members. Offers specific assistance regarding breast cancer, to help stop smoking, and offers literature on other cancers.

Chronic Fatigue Syndrome

NATIONAL CHRONIC FATIGUE AND IMMUNE DISORDERS ASSOCIATION
    800-442-3437

For people affected by chronic fatigue and immunological disorders. Provides free information about Chronic Fatigue Syndrome and referral to local CFS support groups. Also offers a 900-number information line.

Credit Problems

NATIONAL FOUNDATION FOR CONSUMER CREDIT   **800-388-2227**

Refers callers to local chapters of the Consumer Credit Counseling Center which works with persons overburdened by credit-card and other debt.

Trained counselors work with the debtor to establish a debt management plan to pay back creditors and prevent debt problems from recurring. Seeks to involve creditors in the process. Hotline number refers callers to local counselors by area code.

Day Care Dilemmas

CHILD CARE AWARE   **800-424-2246**

This toll-free number links callers to local community-based agencies for assistance in finding quality child care and resources in their community. Callers are advised what child care options exist in their home or work zip code.

Depression

NATIONAL DEPRESSIVE AND MANIC-DEPRESSIVE ASSOCIATION
     800-826-3632

Support and information for persons with depressive and manic-depressive illnesses and their families. Recommends self-help support groups in your area. Also offers an information package on depressive illnesses, a chapter directory, and catalog of books.

DEPRESSION AFTER DELIVERY   **800-944-4773**

Information and support for women suffering from postpartum depression, anxiety, and psychosis. Call this number and leave name and address to receive information.

Diabetes

JUVENILE DIABETES FOUNDATION   **800-223-1138**

Callers are directed to local support groups which provide information regarding local care providers; also provides information regarding the disease and its treatment.

AMERICAN DIABETES ASSOCIATION   **800-232-3472**

Support services for diabetes patients and their families. Chapters provide local support services, including referral information.

AMERICAN DIETETIC ASSOCIATION   **800-366-1655**

Information on proper diet for diabetics, brochures on non-insulin diabetes, infant feeding, and child nutrition.

Divorce

PARENTS WITHOUT PARTNERS   **800-637-7974**

National organization of single parents, primarily for divorced parents. Callers are referred to a local PWP chapter in their zip code area. Support for single parents and their children as well as recreational activities.

Domestic Violence

NATIONAL COALITION AGAINST DOMESTIC VIOLENCE   **800-779-7233**
    (TTD)   **800-787-3224**

A 24-hour crisis line. Offers information and referral to local shelters for victims. Also assistance and information for battered victims' families.

Eating Disorders

NATIONAL ASSOCIATION OF ANOREXIA NERVOSA AND ASSOCIATED
    DISORDERS   **847-831-3438**

Provides information on anorexia, bulimia, and other eating disorders. Trained counselors talk with patients and family members. Provides referrals to self-help groups, therapy, and health-care professionals. Also provides information about community-resource persons who lecture to school groups to educate children on the dangers of eating disorders.

Gambling

GAMBLER'S ANONYMOUS   **213-386-8789**

More than 1,200 chapters nationally. Aims to help compulsive gamblers overcome their addiction through peer-support groups.

Legal Help

Consult your local directory for your community's Legal Aid Society, or contact your town or state's Bar Association and ask for information about "pro bono" legal assistance. Most Bar Associations have a program to provide free (pro bono) legal assistance. Perhaps you qualify, or they may be able to offer you a local referral.

Literacy

NATIONAL INSTITUTE FOR LITERACY HOTLINE   **800-228-8813**

Callers are referred to local literacy programs in their area. Hotline serves both those in need of literacy services as well as volunteers who wish to donate their time as tutors.

Marriage Counseling

ASSOCIATION OF COUPLES FOR MARRIAGE ENRICHMENT   **800-634-8325**

Couples helping couples strengthen their own marriage. Local chapters sponsor support groups, lead retreats, and conduct workshops.

Orphan Diseases

NATIONAL ORGANIZATION FOR RARE DISORDERS, INC.   **800-999-NORD**

Hotline can provide information on what resources are available on rare medical disorders. Also serves as a networking aid, as callers can be put in touch with other persons with the same disorder. Advocates for orphan disease research.

SIDS

SUDDEN INFANT DEATH SYNDROME ALLIANCE   **800-221-SIDS**

A central source of information about Sudden Infant Death Syndrome. Hotline provides referrals to doctors, counseling, and parent-support groups.

Wishes Granted

MAKE A WISH FOUNDATION   **800-722-WISH**

Works to give terminally ill children the life experience of their dreams. Callers to this number are directed to the local chapter in their state.

STARLIGHT FOUNDATION   **800-274-7827**

Also works to give terminally ill children the life experience of their dreams. Provides information on local hospitals' entertainment programs.

Workplace Issues

9 TO 5, NATIONAL ASSOCIATION OF WORKING WOMEN JOB SURVIVAL
    HOTLINE   **800-522-0925**

Job-problem counselors can advise women on how to best deal with specific problems in the workplace. Also offers legislative assistance regarding legislative issues that impact on working women.

Index

About the Author

DEBORAH NORVILLE IS THE ANCHOR of *Inside Edition,* America's top-rated syndicated newsmagazine. The winner of two national Emmy Awards, Norville began her reporting career in Atlanta while still a college student. She reported and anchored local news in Chicago before joining NBC News in New York. A former correspondent for CBS News, Norville also hosted the nationwide *Deborah Norville Show* on radio. She and her husband, Karl Wellner, live with their three children in New York. This is her first book.

Deborah Norville can be reached on the Internet at:
www.dnorville.com